PRAISE FOR

I Hate Everyone . . .
Starting with Me

"More punch lines per paragraph than any book I've read in years."

—*The New York Times*

"Often hilarious, often shocking, totally politically incorrect."

—Liz Smith

"She holds nothing back."

—*The Washington Post*

"Spares no one."

—*The Huffington Post*

"An entertaining rant . . . The only thing missing is the sound of a drumroll and cymbals to feel as though one is sitting in a nightclub watching a live comedy marathon . . . A raucous, biting look at life."

—*Kirkus Reviews*

"Nobody, but nobody, can hate like Joan Rivers. It is a gift. It is also shocking, the things she makes us laugh at . . . Joan Rivers is extraordinary, but she's not for the easily offended—or for anyone who gets offended at all."

—*People*

"Rivers is equally passionate and opinionated on every subject she discusses. Hilarious and undeniably original."

—*Publishers Weekly*

BERKLEY TITLES BY JOAN RIVERS

I Hate Everyone...Starting with Me

Diary of a Mad Diva

DIARY *of a Mad* DIVA

JOAN RIVERS

BERKLEY BOOKS, NEW YORK

THE BERKLEY PUBLISHING GROUP
Published by the Penguin Group
Penguin Group (USA) LLC
375 Hudson Street, New York, New York 10014

USA • Canada • UK • Ireland • Australia • New Zealand • India • South Africa • China

penguin.com

A Penguin Random House Company

Interior photographs: pages 2, 48, 66, 166, and 268 by Aldo Coppelli; pages 30, 112, 138, 184, 212, and 240 by Jocelyn Pickett; page 88 by We tv; pages 172 and 247 by Larry Amoros.

Berkley trade paperback ISBN: 978-0-425-26903-9

The Library of Congress has cataloged the Berkley hardcover edition as follows:

Rivers, Joan.
Diary of a mad diva / Joan Rivers. — First edition.
pages cm
ISBN 978-0-425-26902-2
1. Rivers, Joan—Diaries. 2. Comedians—United States—Diaries. I. Title.
PN2287.R55A3 2014
792.702'8092—dc23
[B]
2014015870

PUBLISHING HISTORY
Berkley hardcover edition / July 2014
Berkley trade paperback edition / April 2015

PRINTED IN THE UNITED STATES OF AMERICA

10 9 8 7 6 5 4 3 2 1

Cover design by Rita Frangie.
Interior text design by Pauline Neuwirth.

This diary was written to the best of Joan Rivers's memory. As such, some of the events may not be 100 percent . . . or even 5 percent factually correct. Miss Rivers is, after all, 235 years old, and frequently mistakes her daughter, Melissa, for the actor Laurence Fishburne.

Miss Rivers wrote this diary as a comedic tome, not unlike *Saving Private Ryan* or *The Bell Jar.* While Miss Rivers doesn't really like skinny models and actresses, she doesn't actually believe that they're all bulimics and they all carry buckets instead of purses. Similarly, she doesn't really think that all Germans are anti-Semitic Nazi sympathizers, that all Mexican Americans tunneled in across the border, that all celebrities are drug addicts, shoplifters or closet cases, or that Noah built his ark with non-union labor.

Miss Rivers does, however, believe that anyone who takes anything in this book seriously is an idiot. And she says if anyone has a problem with that they can feel free to call her lawyer, Clarence Darrow.

Sometimes people write novels and they just be so wordy and so self-absorbed. . . . I am a proud non-reader of books.

—KANYE WEST (Reuters, May 2009)

This book be dedicated to Kanye West,
because he'll never fuckin' read it.

JANUARY

Fuck Lamaze. You try downing a bottle of barbies with a dry throat.

JANUARY 1

Dear Diary:

This diary is my Christmas gift from Melissa and Cooper and I'm more disappointed than I was on my wedding night when I found out that Edgar was half Chinese—and not the good half. And this diary's not even from a good store. I was hoping for at least a Cartier watch. I wouldn't even have minded if it was spelled with a K. I know, it's Christmas season and we're Jewish and we shouldn't care about gifts, but if indeed we did kill Christ—and I'm not saying we did; for all we know he could have slipped and fallen onto that cross (maybe he was clumsy; maybe he drank)—then something's got to ease the guilt. And the more expensive that something is, the less guilty I feel.

Anyhow, this is a new book for a new year and I'm feeling great. To celebrate, I got matching vagina piercings with my two best girlfriends, Margie Stern and Brucey Jenner.

I'm writing this in Mexico. On the spur of the moment, Melissa, Cooper and I decided to fly down here, and we were right: It's a perfect way to ring in the New Year—great resort, private beach and plenty of servants who'll do anything for a thirty-cent tip. This place is kind of like Downton Abbey with sombreros. Last night I got an eight-hour pedicure from Maria while resting my feet on her "brother," Jose, who was crouched over like a footstool. I let him switch positions every two hours so he wouldn't cramp and, more importantly, so Maria wouldn't slip and accidentally paint my ankles dusty coral. Unfortunately I can't take credit for the position-switching thing; I got the idea by watching *Amistad* on cable last week. I think if the ship's captain had let the slaves switch sides every couple of days not only would they have rowed faster but they would have had the strength to make faces at Anthony Hopkins.

This morning when I woke up and looked out my window, there was Conchita, out in the field threshing wheat so that her "brother," Juan, would be able to make me toast for my morning breakfast. I appreciate all of my south-of-the-border neighbors' semi-hard work and hope they've stolen enough loose change and shiny trinkets from my bureau so that when they get caught trying to tunnel into America next month, they'll have money to pay a mediocre deportation lawyer.

JANUARY 2

Dear Diary:

I haven't kept a diary in years. The last time I kept one I had just come back from a girls-only weekend with Eleanor Roosevelt and her best friend, Gayle. We all giggled that girls are better than guys, and then we douched with Gatorade and wrist-wrestled till we fell asleep.

I wasn't planning on keeping a journal this time, but when I told my friend Bambi I was going to Mexico for the New Year, she said, "Oh, you ought to keep a diary, like whatshername did . . . oh, like Anne Frank did." Like Anne Frank did???? Did you read Anne Frank's diary??? What a bitch Bambi has turned out to be, to compare me to Anne Frank! I've written six books, and Anne? She didn't even complete her one. She's no writer. Did you ever read her book? She has no ending! "Uh-oh! The Nazis are coming up the . . ."

I'm trying to forgive Bambi; it's been such a long friendship. I knew her way back when she was still Bernice, before the electrolysis, the implants, the Restylane and the glass eye that almost works. I forgave her bitterness. She turned the day her husband, Ernie, a prominent Long Island orthodontist, left her for a fifty-three-year-old Little League coach/Boy Scout leader with a severe overbite. Until this we were friends, but to compare me to Anne Frank? Who the fuck does she think she is? I'm nothing like Anne Frank. She lived in a walk-up; I live in a penthouse. And unlike Anne Frank, I *do* things: I go out. I shop. I go to the theater. I get *professional* haircuts. I'm way up there and I'm a gal on the go; Anne Frank was fifteen and that lazy bitch played the shut-in card for more than two years. No, Bambi, if I keep a diary it won't be like Anne Frank's; just for openers, it'll be in English.

JANUARY 3

Dear Diary:

Trouble started today with AT&T. I hate AT&T. It obviously stands for Always Terrible Transmission. I tried to call the States and couldn't, so I called AT&T about my international phone service, which sucks more than Monica Lewinsky under a White House desk, and I got a recording that told me "a disabled war veteran will answer your call." Great. I have to complain about my long-distance bill to Private Jimmy, who lost his face, ass and limbs in Tora Bora. "I'm sorry you're a torso on a dolly, Private First Class Jimmy, but does that mean for the rest of my life I have to pay an extra $6 for data roaming?"

What do you say when they hit you with "a disabled vet will try to give you a hand"? Do you chance it and answer, "Does he have one?" I hate being put in awkward positions, like the utter disappointment I felt after I did a benefit performance for thalidomide adults and no one applauded. To this day I'm not sure whether the silence was because they couldn't clap or because they didn't like me.

Anyhow, I did what any American would do: sent a check to Wounded Warriors, hung up on the mother-fucker, and switched to Verizon.

JANUARY 4

Dear Diary:

Something about Anne Frank's story kept bothering me and I finally figured out what. It's not that she wasn't pretty; a lot of girls aren't pretty and they still do okay, right, Avril Lavigne? But Anne just didn't try. How would it have hurt the woman who slipped her food when the Nazis weren't looking to have included a lipstick, an eye shadow and, God knows, a concealer? The girl had nothing but time on her hands. Would it have killed Anne to take a couple of minutes out of her "busy" day and throw on a little blush? And there's something else I just can't make sense out of. With all of that "me time" available, why didn't Anne's mother redecorate? You can do a lot with blackout curtains if you're willing to strain your brain a little and think outside the box. Hopefully the answer will come to me before Passover. I'd hate to interrupt the Seder by adding a fifth question: "Were there no throw pillows in all of Amsterdam?"

JANUARY 5

Dear Diary:

We've been down here almost a week and I'm beginning to realize the Mexicans are not a swell-looking people. Not all Mexicans, just the Mayan-influenced staff working here at the resort. They have no necks. Perhaps it's because they spent all those years carrying heavy stones on their heads to build their gloomy and useless temples. Their heads look like pumpkins sitting on washing machines. I don't say this in a judgmental, pejorative way; I say it in a capitalistic way, because frankly, I have a jewelry line, and if they have no necks that means they can't buy necklaces and that means that my beloved Cooper might have to go to some cheap community college, or worse, join the Peace Corps and work for free—for free!—helping other people who have no necks.

JANUARY 6

Dear Diary:

Watching the news. Today was the anniversary of two of the biggest events in American history: Nancy Kerrigan getting clubbed in the knee in 1994, and Congress giving the 2000 election to George W. Bush. My world was changed on that fateful day, and since then I've never been able to watch figure skating the same way. Up until then I always thought of figure skating as something gay men who were tone-deaf and couldn't sing in piano bars did to pass their time, but it turns out I was wrong. Figure skating is something needy women with thin lips and big thighs do to pass their time. Innocence lost.

JANUARY 7

Dear Diary:

Today was our travel day back to New York. The airport was packed and I felt a little guilty as we jumped the line. And Melissa didn't help; she's actually getting quite verbal and testy every time I hop into a wheelchair and make her push me past the pregnant women and sick children. She also says that my little act of rolling my eyes back and shivering and plucking at people's chests and whispering, "Say a prayer for me, *amigo*. The prognosis doesn't look *bueno*," is a little over the top. I know it upsets her, but boy does it work like a charm.

I then try to make sure I'm not stuck sitting next to some chatty asshole. But I'm prepared. I have six Ambien and an intentionally open purse filled with Massengill, Vagisil, Preparation H, a copy of my will, and books on Amelia Earhart and Pan Am Flight 103's surprise landing in Lockerbie.

JANUARY 8

Dear Diary:

One last thing about Anne Frank's diary that was bothering me: the Nazis—and *their* sloppy work ethic. Anne and her entire posse were hidden behind a bookcase for two years and no one found them? Do you know what that means? Nobody ever cleaned or dusted the bookcase, that's what it means! I know there was a war going on and maybe nobody had time to do a white-glove test, but seriously, how much work would it have been to casually walk by with a feather duster or a Swiffer? I find the whole thing shocking; and the thing that shocks me the most is my housekeeper obviously used to be a Nazi.

JANUARY 9

Dear Diary:

Our Mexican vacation is over and I'm back in rainy New York. I met my friend Margie for lunch, and in the six blocks from my house to the restaurant, I got splashed on, shoved, banged into and told to "go fuck myself" in three different languages. And just as I was entering the restaurant, I got shit on by a pigeon. It feels so good to be home.

JANUARY 10

Dear Diary:

I am shaking. This morning I did *The Howard Stern Show* and it was the most amazing experience I've ever had on the show. I must've been a guest on his show a hundred times, but today was the first time ever, ever, ever, in all these years, that Howard never once used the words "penis," "vagina," "midget" or "retard." It wasn't until later that I found out it was because he had a sore throat. In retaliation, this was the first time I never, never, never once used the words "cuntface," "turd burglar" or "Palin."

JANUARY 11

Dear Diary:

Flew to L.A. today to get back to work on *Fashion Police.* I didn't realize how much I adore taping it. It's been almost a month since I insulted celebrities, shamed lesbos and made fat jokes about Aretha Franklin. I need my fix!

JANUARY 12

Dear Diary:

I spent half the day in the car schlepping all over L.A. going from meeting to meeting, ass-kissing to ass-kissing. My driver listens to the top-rated oldies radio station in L.A., KRTH. It was fun listening for a while, but the station played the same Eddie Money songs over and over and over and over and over again, all day long. No matter where I was in L.A. or what time of day it was, when I got in the car they were playing Eddie.

I figure since 1960 there must be 100,000 songs to choose from, yet KRTH plays Eddie Money over and over, like an autistic man-child who has to wear a helmet just to eat cereal. I have nothing against Eddie Money; he seems like a lovely man. I met him once a few years ago; he was my waiter at Denny's. But why is KRTH playing him all day, all the time? Is Eddie related to the station owner? Does Eddie have blackmail photos of the program manager fucking a goat? I don't understand it. There are 3.8 million people living in Los Angeles; do any of them call up KRTH every morning and say, "If you don't play an Eddie Money song at least fifty-eight times today I'm going to kill myself"? What I *could* understand is if they called up and said, "If you *do* play Justin Bieber even once, I'm going to kill you."

I wouldn't mind listening to Eddie Money all the time—or even Justin Bieber—if KRTH would just mix it up a little. Throw in an Anne Murray song every now and then. Even if you don't like her, her songs are good for the listener. They work as a natural Valium. Or something nostalgic, like Jennifer Holliday's first hit, "I Am Not Dieting."

JANUARY 13

Dear Diary:

Cooper is totally into lacrosse, so Melissa and I went to his game today. He was very good. At least I think he was. I don't know what lacrosse is about. All I saw was a bunch of thirteen-year-old boys with sticks and helmets furiously whipping a rock-hard ball at a kid with no shin pads (and no teeth) standing in front of a net.

Later: Googled "lacrosse." It's a French-Canadian word. It means "beat the shit out of the goalie."

JANUARY 14

Dear Diary:

Red-eyed in from L.A. Found myself sitting next to someone who was the spitting image of my cousin Leon. And I say "spitting image" because he was spitting. (And shaking. And twitching.) Every time this guy spit he washed down the seats of not only the people in front of us, but also the people in first class. I haven't been that wet since I went through menopause. I couldn't sleep, and sleep is important—just ask Sunny von Bülow. Which is why I always request to sit next to Stephen Hawking. He doesn't toss and turn, and his keeper, God bless her, wipes off not only his spit, but dries off the entire cabin. There's even another bonus: The rhythmic hum of his ventilator can be so soothing it helps me go into REM sleep!

But back to the idiot next to me. I was about to say something like, "Calm down, Blinky, a lot of people are nervous about flying," but the stewardess mouthed to me, "He has Parkinson's." I signaled back, "What? He has what? Parking problems? He likes *Parks and Recreation*? He's a Parker Posey fan?" Then she did a little hopping, trembling motion until I got it. I didn't bother to say hello to him because (a) I could tell he was an upgrade, and (b) his wardrobe told me he had absolutely no juice in show business.

To top it all off, this guy was really aloof. You'd think anybody who took ten minutes to buckle a seat belt because of the Parkinson's would be friendly. I mean, how many friends could he have? Other than the FEMA earthquake management experts, who could put up with all the shaking without getting nauseous? The stewardess had to take Dramamine before she came over to serve him. All night long his head bobbed up and down more than a ten-year-old sitting in Michael Jackson's lap. It's now three o'clock in the morning, I'm trying to sleep, and I swear to God he is kicking and thrashing like a Filipino day laborer trying to get out of Kathie Lee's sweatshop. At one point I asked to buy him a drink and he said, "Martini." I said, "Shaken or stirred?" The dumb fuck didn't even get the joke.

JANUARY 17

Dear Diary:

I'm back in L.A. visiting Melissa, and tonight I went with my agent, Steve Levine, to a semi-important dinner party in Beverly Hills. And I say "semi-important" because if it were really important he would've taken Chris Rock or Jimmy Fallon or JWoww. And I know it was semi-important because there were only three or four people there who could help my career, and they could only do that if they called in a favor to someone more important than themselves. In Australia. I'm not complaining however; last week he took Kathy Griffin to an all-you-can-eat buffet at an Olive Garden.

Gayle King was at the dinner party, looking quite feminine and sporting a small tattoo of Gertrude Stein on her left wrist. I made the usual small talk with her, like, "You and Charlie Rose have such great chemistry," and "Your new high-collared dresses really hide your large, mannish shoulders." And she seemed delighted as she smiled and walked away. But what I really wanted to say to her was, "What's Oprah's private number? I want to crank call her."

And while I'm on the subject, Charlie Rose—who I like to think of as a good, good friend—once came to a dinner party at my house with Amanda Burden, his longtime lady love. I adore them both. I saw a new friendship starting: Sunday-night screenings, meeting at the dog run, sharing a house in Mexico . . . I guess they didn't see it the same way because I never heard from them again. In fact, Charlie turned down the opportunity to narrate a PBS special I had written on anti-Semitism called *Stop Bothering the Hebes*.

JANUARY 18

Dear Diary:

Exhausted. Just came back from yet another party, this time with Steve Levine's assistant, Jackie. I'm starting to know how bacteria feel on the food chain. I was the oldest person in the room. They were all young hip actor types who made no eye contact with me. Is this generational or just rude? In my day, people made eye contact. Take John Wayne Gacy, for example. Good mood or bad, bless him, he made eye contact. Even at his busiest moments, like when he was waterproofing his crawl space, he always found time to look you right in the eyes and say, "What'd you do today, Joan? Tell some jokes, sell some jewelry on QVC, just hang with your peeps and smoke a little blunt?" instead of being self-involved and saying, "I was very busy: I drank a six-pack, made some clown paintings and fucked my cell mate. Care for some more punch?"

JANUARY 19

Dear Diary:

I'm really upset!! I finally got into the apartment of my blind neighbor, Esther Mortman (I slipped past her while she was groping for her tennis racquet . . . Who's she kidding?), and I was right! She *does* have a park view! This kills me. Why, why, why should blind people have apartments with park views? I don't want to say anything negative about Esther even though she's a lousy dresser. Checks and plaids together? Time and time again I chide her, "C'mon, Esther, what's with this outfit, are you blind? Ooops." But as I suspected, she doesn't even appreciate her view; just to aggravate me she purposely places her easy chair facing the wall. As

I said, I don't want to say anything because I really like Esther. She's so independent, for years I didn't even know she was blind; I thought she was just a stuck-up cunt who never gave me a compliment like, "Have you lost weight? New hairdo?"

JANUARY 20

Dear Diary:

It's Melissa's birthday. Thirty-nine years ago tonight I was screaming, "Get this out of me!" And thirty-nine years plus nine months ago I was screaming the same thing. It was an easy birth and I remember my joy when my obstetrician answered yes to the following questions: Is she breathing? Is she healthy? Is she white?

On the way to Melissa's party I ran into Wolf Blitzer and he broke my aura; he was *right in my face* when he growled at me. We were practically conjoined. (It made me think: Do people have to represent their names? Be careful what you name your kids. You could be jinxing the little motherfuckers. What if Sunny gets a job as a guard in a concentration camp? What if Goldie has black roots? What if Lucky has one eye, cradle cap and an open spine? Nice job, Mom. I always wanted to ask Gwyneth Paltrow, "Does Apple have worms?")

I said to Wolf, "Wolf, unless you're a dentist removing a molar or my Melissa trying to get my jewelry off of me before I'm dead, there's no reason for you to be this close. And don't give me that 'what if we're kissing?'

crap. You and I both know a hooker will fuck you, suck you, put things up your ass and call you dirty names, but she'll never, *ever* kiss you. Especially if your name is Wolf." Then as he was walking away I said to him, "Yo, Shorty, have a nice day, and by the way, who the fuck named you Wolf? Looking at you, so many other names come to mind: Raccoon, Ferret-Face, Llama-Puss or just a simple, right-to-the-point No-Chin." (There's nothing I hate worse than a person with no chin. When they get old they're just going to be a neck and a smile.)

JANUARY 21

Dear Diary:

Wolf isn't the only person who's in your face all the time. Take that narcissistic loser Tyra Banks. Tyra's always standing up for herself and her "race" over perceived slights. For example, she'll say, "You just pushed me because I'm black!" No, I pushed you because the train was coming right at you, you bulimic twit.

JANUARY 22

Dear Diary:

Just got another no for my PBS special, *Stop Bothering the Hebes*. John Galliano said, "*Non.*" I think I'm going to sic Jerry Lewis on him.

Just finished watching President Obama's inauguration. (I TiVoed it because last night I was watching the premiere episode of *The Price Is Right* with Winona Ryder.) The president's speech was okay. The "we're all in this together" stuff plus the usual "we're all Americans" and the ever-popular "we're all equal" shit went over very well. I like the first two sentiments but boy oh boy is Obie wrong on number three. We're *not* all equal. I've seen nude photos of Tommy Lee *and* Bruce Lee, and no amount of legislation is gonna level that playing field. Tommy wins ten to one. Poor Bruce Lee. As Confucius say, "Be happy with a mini. Could be worse; could be an innie." I feel so sorry for Asian men; not once in my nearly two hundred years on this planet have I ever heard the Asian woman who lives next door to me yell out, in a fit of unbridled lust, "Oh, Hop Sing, give it to me, baby! Punish me with your huge yellow tool!" Not once. Usually what I hear her say is, "Is it in?"

Back to the inauguration. I watched it at home and the television coverage sucked. First they'd show President Obama in front of the Capitol making a speech after taking the oath of office. And then during his speech they kept cutting to smiling black people in the audience. Then they'd go back to Obama for a minute and then cut back to three or four other smiling black people. There were over 900,000 people on the Mall watching the inauguration; what are the odds they were *all* smiling black people? If I want to see millions of smiling black people, I'll set up a camera in the hallway outside Kim Kardashian's bedroom.

I resent that the networks think we're so shallow, that because the president is black they have to keep doing cutaways only to smiling black people in the audience. If Chris Christie ever becomes president, will they only cut to Kathy Bates chewing and burping?

I wish Obama would have livened the speech up a bit; given the crowd a wink, a smile, a bad-boy hip thrust. His biggest offense was that the speech was boring. How great would it have been if he said, "Good news, gang! My daughter Sasha's expecting! She's gonna be eating government cheese for two! And even better, Hillary's the baby daddy!"

JANUARY 23

Dear Diary:

Just heard how my cleaning lady, Chiquita, enjoyed the inauguration. Apparently everybody in the country was invited to it except me. But I'm not upset. In my time, I've slept with many a president. There was Teddy Roosevelt, who was some little roughrider. I had a major, major affair with FDR, who, by the way, had a coupla fetishes. He used to say, "C'mon, Joan, you be a hot nurse and I'll play a little cripple boy who needs a sponge bath." And I don't want to rehash this bit of history here, but it's common knowledge that Abe Lincoln and I were an item. And FYI, A.L. would've been alive today if he had just listened to me. I begged that little fairy boy (everyone knows he was gay. C'mon—shawl, stovepipe hat, a darkened mole. Obvious!) not to go to the theater. I said, "Stay home in bed with me. We'll decoupage and watch Lifetime TV movies." And he said, "Nope! I want to go to the theater! *Les Miz* is playing, and Fantine, before they pull out her teeth, is quite the looker in a clever little A-line and matching open-toed shoes." The rest is history.

JANUARY 24

Dear Diary:

I had dinner tonight with my friend Cindy Adams, and it was great. Since Cindy's a famous gossip columnist, there's never a check because the chefs want to be on her good side. So I get the latest dirt *and* a free meal. We're not lesbians, but if I could mooch steak and lobster off of Cindy every night, I'd learn to build bookcases, play golf and make her my gal pal. What I like about Cindy is that in her column she tells the truth. If I had a column, I'd lie or do a lot of "blind items" so I couldn't get sued: things like, "Which five-foot-seven Scientologist was seen standing on a box trying on a muumuu in Forgotten Woman?" Or, "Which fifty-year-old star who used to be married to Ashton K. was seen at a playground asking little boys if their testicles had dropped yet?" Or, "Which blond British singer stopped rolling in the deep long enough to break into a Dunkin' Donuts in desperate need of a fix? And then had to spend the night in the clink because even though she was allowed one phone call, her mouth was too full to be understood?"

JANUARY 25

Dear Diary:

Flew from L.A. to New York last night and had a terrible headache until Vonda, my favorite flight attendant, gave me some good dirt. Anne Hathaway is a regular on Vonda's flight, and Vonda said that Anne eats *everything* on board and then spends the rest of the flight in the bathroom purging and vomiting and singing, not that I could tell the difference. Vonda said Anne's vomiting really upset Natalie Portman, who was in 2F. "This is terrible, terrible," she kept saying. "That hag is hogging the bathroom. Now *I'm* going to have to puke in my purse!"

JANUARY 26

Dear Diary:

Still thinking about Anne Hathaway. I don't understand how she won an Oscar for *Les Miz*; she was only in the movie for five minutes. It was a great performance, but I say again, it was only five minutes. If they're going to give an Oscar for a great five-minute performance then they should award it posthumously to Jackie Kennedy. She wowed me in the Zapruder film. Boy oh boy, that bitch knew how to steal a scene. Forget that Anne Hathaway acted and sang, Jackie did it with no dialogue at all! JFK's flying gray matter was incidental. The eye never left Jackie in her pink suit crawling out of that convertible.

JANUARY 27

Dear Diary:

> **Q: What's sweaty, lonely and weighs ten thousand pounds?**
> A: The front row of a Donny Osmond concert.

I went to a Donny Osmond concert last night. Got in free, which means I had to stand up in the audience and wave and hear their happy whispers about me, like, "She looks older," "Check out the hump," "Why does that Jew comic have a better seat than me?" etc., etc. Anyhow, he was fantastic! I had a great time, and not just because he put on such a wonderful show, but because in my entire life I've never felt prettier. I felt like Marilyn on *The Munsters*. The only negative was I didn't know whether to offer the woman sitting next to me breath mints or peanuts. I fully expected Jack Hanna to walk in, clap his hands and suddenly have the entire mezzanine start grooming themselves and hurling feces. (Donny, who is no chicken himself, did the show without an intermission; maybe he figured if he took a break they'd never come back from the snack bar.) But to be perfectly honest, there *is* something special about seeing 2,200 wildly unattractive, morbidly obese older women singing and wetting their diapers to "Puppy Love."

This doesn't just happen at Donny Osmond concerts. Try going to a Joni Mitchell concert these days: Fistfights no longer break out with those old dykes; they barely have the energy to push and shove when Joni sings songs from *Blue*, which these days refers to their legs. The fans are just getting older, and this includes my audiences too, some of whom think the Carson show is still on (and some are referring to Kit). Instead of hearing "Bravo," I hear "What did she say?" followed by "I don't get it" and "I feel damp, Lenny, let's go."

JANUARY 28

Dear Diary:

I was thinking about the Donny Osmond show again. Nobody in the audience was dressed up. I understand that spandex can only do so much, but make an effort when you're at a show. Just because you're watching *War Horse* doesn't mean you should smell like one. The only people who can get away with not dressing up for a concert are Andrea Bocelli fans. But if, God forbid, his sight comes back while he's onstage, he might take one look and pull an Oedipus.

Speaking of dressing up, I spent tonight watching a football game with Cooper. The camera swung around to the stands and showed a whole group of grown businessmen wearing uniforms with players' names on them. Staring directly into the camera was a slovenly, bald, three-hundred-pound proctologist from Newark, New Jersey, wearing a Tom Brady jersey. I wanted to shout at the screen, "Are you Tom Brady? Because if you are you've really let yourself go." Why do men do this? Do they consider it a form of homage? If so, shouldn't Tom Brady go to his proctologist's office wearing a plastic glove covered in Vaseline?

JANUARY 29

Dear Diary:

It's the middle of Award Season in Hollywood, which is as important to actors as Ramadan is to Muslims. In fact, if a Dutch cartoonist ever drew a cartoon mocking the Oscar ceremony, I guarantee you there would be a violent jihad in front of Spago. And it won't even be pretty to look at because no one is allowed to dress up anymore during Award Season. The networks have new decency guidelines which insist that no more breasts, buttocks or genitalia show. Luckily, because of celebrities like Pharrell and his stupid hat, we'll still be able to see assholes.

JANUARY 30

Dear Diary:

Nowadays there are so many award shows: the Golden Globes, the Grammys, the SAGs, the Oscars . . . There are more awards to honor actors than there are stretch marks on Ricky Martin's mouth. And I don't watch to see who wins. As a matter of fact, I don't give a shit who wins; I'm much more interested in who *loses*. I love to watch how the losers mask their reactions when their name is not announced. I can't describe the feelings of joy I get watching narcissistic actors pretending to be happy for someone else. I tingle all over; I imagine this must be what a person in desperate need of an organ transplant feels when they hear the good news of a fatal twelve-car pileup not three blocks from their hospice bed.

The red carpet is a special place to me; it's where I spent my formative wonder years—thirty-five to sixty-seven. It's magical; where else can an everyday, regular, simple hausfrau like me meet rich, famous superstars fresh out of rehab and grill them about their sobriety coach, their life coach and their meditation coach, or ask them if they have any idea when their tremors, teeth grinding and night sweats will stop? Where else can A-list actresses show off the $3 million necklaces they've borrowed or the four thousand African children they've bought and will love until they reach puberty and the problems start? And where else, other than on Bravo, can no-talent has-beens parade around, twirling and posing as though anyone in the audience knows or gives a shit who they are?

Working on red carpets is not new to me. My daughter, Melissa, and I have been on more of them than Aladdin, but what I like about them is they give me the chance to be a part of the excitement without actually having to watch the tedious shows themselves. Who needs to watch Catherine Zeta-Jones lip-sync or James Franco sleepwalk or Ben Stiller do anything? No! No! No! (I sound like I did on my wedding night.) I'm a busy woman. My time could be better spent writing jokes, designing jewelry or cruising Craigslist searching for an eighty-year-old man who has eighty million in the bank and eighty days to live.

JANUARY 31

Dear Diary:

Today is Carol Channing's birthday. If she were alive, she'd be 192. I idolize her. Whenever she sang "Hello, Dolly!" she brought the house down. Unfortunately it was the only thing she did well. But many stars only do one thing well: Ginger Rogers could dance backwards; David Copperfield can make a motorcycle disappear. And of course the best one-trick pony is Kristen Stewart, who got a whole career by being able to juggle directors' balls. These people don't have a broad skill set, like Ted Bundy, for example. Ted was a lawyer, a student, a model; he liked baseball, football, fishing; he drove a car, he slaughtered co-eds. He was a real jack-of-all-trades. I hear that on his way to the electric chair he sang a rousing rendition of "Don't Rain on My Parade," à la Carol, and in an homage to Ginger, he tapped backwards the entire way to Old Sparky.

P.S. My assistant, Jocelyn, just told me that Carol Channing may still be alive. Whatever.

FEBRUARY

The Backstreet Boys have not aged well.

FEBRUARY 1

Dear Diary:

Just the other day my dearest, closest, dare I say best friend, Goldie Hall—I mean Hawn—asked me, "Joan, you battered old crone, what does 'red-carpet style' mean?" I told her, "Goldalah, you delusional hag, red-carpet style is like herpes: You either have it or you don't. Or as another one of my close BFFs Lou Ann Rhymes says, 'You have to be born with red-carpet style. You can't steal it from someone else'—like a husband." If you're Aretha Franklin, "style" means looking great while sweating mayonnaise through sixty yards of organza. For most actresses, red-carpet style means expensive earrings, designer gowns and the opportunity to make fun of all the big, fat girls who have to squeeze into a size two. But never mind the gowns and the accessories, the most important thing to wear on the red carpet is kneepads. Just like basic black, every starlet knows you can never go wrong in kneepads. As the first lady of American theater once said to me (and I'm talking about Helen Hayes, not Neil Patrick Harris), "You never know when you'll need them: You could pass out from the heat, you might collapse because you mistimed your drugs, or—talk about luck—you might suddenly find yourself alone with Steven Spielberg."

I'm not saying it's so (and in fact, I don't believe it), but one of the great Hollywood myths is that Liam Neeson hadn't had a decent role in years when he ran into Spielberg on a red carpet. One men's room and twenty minutes later, he's Oskar Schindler saving any Jew who was good at making pots and pans.

My favorite red-carpet look of all time was worn by Tatum O'Neal. She was ten years old and dressed in a tuxedo. She was adorable. Winning that Oscar was just the first of many wins. She went on to win day passes, conjugal visits, time off for good behavior and occasional partial custody of some of her kids.

How You Can Tell It's Award Season in Hollywood

1. You can't get an appointment with any plastic surgeon in Beverly Hills for the three months prior.
2. All the ladies' rooms smell of vomit.
3. All the leading men suddenly show up with beards . . . on their arms.

FEBRUARY 2

Dear Diary:

Today is Groundhog Day, which is a holiday celebrating a brownish, bucktoothed rat. The old wives' tale is that if the groundhog sticks his head out of the ground and sees his shadow, we'll have six more weeks of winter. Great, it's better than having Sam Champion stick his head out of his boyfriend's ass to see if we're going to have six more weeks of *Glee*.

FEBRUARY 3

Dear Diary:

My assistant, Jocelyn, just walked in, saw me writing and said, "Are you aware it's 2 p.m.? Get up. We have to change the sheets." She's so rude and it's my own fault. I should hire illegals. You can slap 'em around and who are they going to complain to? Not the police. (It's a win-win, except on Cinco de Mayo, when they get cheeky.)

FEBRUARY 4

Dear Diary:

Happy Birthday, Rosa Parks! In her memory, I decided to sit all the way in the back of my limo on the way home tonight. Rosa was such a pioneer. She refused to give up her seat to a white person. Truth be told, she refused to give up her seat to anyone, black, white, yellow, red, octoroon . . . People think Rosa was such a rebel; she wasn't. She didn't plant her ass on the seat and not move because she was making a point; she didn't move because she was fucking lazy. Did you ever hear about her doing anything else? Did you ever read a headline that said "Rosa Parks Finds Cure for Juvenile Diabetes"? Or "Rosa Parks Wins *Celebrity Apprentice*"? Or "Rosa Parks Hits Thirty-Six Home Runs for the Dodgers"? No. Rosa just sat. And sat and sat and sat. But, as I said at the beginning of this entry, she *was* a pioneer; she opened the door for generations of lazy people to walk through and sit the fuck down.

FEBRUARY 5

Dear Diary:

Just finished watching *Jeopardy!* It's college week. Hated it. If I want to see a brainy nerd who can't get laid, I'd look at my old class pictures. The only thing worse than *College Jeopardy!* is *Celebrity Jeopardy!* where the questions are so dumbed down Honey Boo Boo could win the fucking game. On the retarded food chain, *Celebrity Jeopardy!* ranks just below *Wheel of Fortune* and *The Real Housewives of Atlanta*. Tom Brokaw is so stupid he lost all of his money when they asked him to spell "mom" backwards.

FEBRUARY 6

Dear Diary:

Left a long message for Prince Charles today. I know he must be depressed because today is the anniversary of his mother becoming queen, and she ain't abdicating anytime soon. Elizabeth has spent more time on the throne than a bulimic at a cabbage convention. Poor PC. Whenever I see him drive by on his way to the mall I shout out advice to make him feel better. When he rolls his eyes I know it's a secret signal between us that he's saying "thank you." I'd love to buy him a small country just so he could have some fun ruling and get a chance to behead people before it's too late. As far as I'm concerned, nothing says "pick-me-up" quite like decapitating an illegal. Am I wrong? Right now Chaz doesn't even have the power to fire the sous chef for not washing his hands after leaving the bathroom.

FEBRUARY 7

Dear Diary:

My friend Larry just sent me multiple pictures of his dog on the stupid dog's birthday. There was Rover in a birthday hat in front of a cake shaped like a bone, and I'm supposed to comment. Frankly, I don't fucking care. If I want to see a dog wearing nothing but a hat, hunched over a bone, I'll look at a Kathy Bates sex tape. People are just nuts over their dogs. Why? Does Larry expect me to buy a gift for that four-legged asshole? What would I buy him and what does he need? I think anyone who can lick his own balls has enough. Just ask Gary Busey. (That's why he's always smiling.) Why do people think we care about their dogs? And an even more pressing question: Why do they think a four-hundred-pound mastiff looks good in a cardboard birthday hat? Even Dr. Phil would look better. Okay, he wouldn't, but almost every other human being would. The only way I'd be interested in Larry's dog is if the dog had Larry's father's eyes.

FEBRUARY 8

Dear Diary:

Watching HBO today and I forgot that February is Black History Month. In honor of it, tomorrow I think I'll hold up a liquor store and fuck me a white woman. And when the police shoot me and turn me over, I'll have on a shirt with a picture of Sasha and Malia to show how far we've come.

FEBRUARY 9

Dear Diary:

Dinner tonight with my friends Sue and Amy. Went to a seafood restaurant. A guy at the next table kept nagging the waiter: "This place smells fishy." Of course it's fishy, you asshole; it's fish! The only time you should ever ask "Is it fishy?" is if you're going down on Rosie O'Donnell.

FEBRUARY 10

Dear Diary:

Today is the Chinese New Year. It's the year of the snake. Michael Fassbender must be thrilled. The New Year celebration is a very important holiday because the Chinese are a very traditional people—to this day they always put extra starch in my shirts, and all of my clothes are neatly folded and boxed, not draped over a hanger like a pregnant hooker in an alley.

I did a little research on this topic, and by "research" I mean I tied my maid Pingpong to a parking meter and made her tell me everything she knew about the Chinese culture. The fact that Pingpong is Filipino and knows nothing of China means zilch to me. I have a great quest for knowledge. One of the interesting facts she spewed out was that the Chinese New Year began with a fight against a mythical beast named Nian, who, on the first day of the New Year, would come into town to eat livestock, crops, villagers and even children. The same exact thing happened on the Jewish New Year, except our mythical beast was named Lainie Kazan and the town she came to was Las Vegas.

FEBRUARY 11

Dear Diary:

Today will go down as a very big day in Homo History: First, the United States military announced it will provide the same benefits to same-sex couples as it does to heterosexual couples, which means sexual assault is now legal for the gays, too! Second, two of my gay friends, Lenny and Denny,* are getting married and they've asked me to marry them. I am thrilled. Not because I get to

* Denny's real name is Milton Glick, but he likes to be called Denny because it rhymes with Lenny and because they both love the metered whimsy of Sondheim and Cole Porter.

conduct their service, but because I get to attend their wedding and don't have to buy a gift. They're getting married on Valentine's Day, which is only three days away—I hope it's not because they have to.

FEBRUARY 12

Dear Diary:

Call me Reverend Joan! Spent a couple of hours online and I am now a proudly ordained minister in the Universal Life Church. The Universal Life Church is a semi-non-denominational church and the church of choice for lesbians who want to get married (usually on their second date, when they've finished bowling). The church doesn't cater to any specific religion such as Christian, Muslim or Jewish, so I never have to mention the names of the leaders of the Big Three: Jesus, Allah and Mandy Patinkin.

FEBRUARY 13

Dear Diary:

I finally finished writing the marriage vows I have to administer tomorrow. I tried to find a gentle balance between passion and grace:

> We are gathered here together to witness the exchanging of marriage vows between Lenny Goldberg and his furrier, Denny Glick.

If there is anyone present today who knows of any reason why this couple should not be married—other than both sets of parents, thirty-seven states, most worldwide religions and the offensive line of the Miami Dolphins—let them speak now or forever hold their peace.

Do you, Lenny, solemnly swear to take Denny to be your lawfully wedded, versatile bottom? Do you promise to love, honor, cherish and keep him for as long as you both shall live, or until he gets Alzheimer's and you can void the prenup and get everything in your name?

Do you, Denny, agree to the same stuff except that if things don't work out you get the cats and he gets the Lady Gaga CDs?

Denny, as a symbol of your promise to Lenny, please place the ruby slippers on his feet, click your heels three times and say, "There's no place like homo, there's no place like homo, there's no place like homo."

Inasmuch as you have consented to be united in the bonds of matrimony—not to mention tied to the bedposts with ball gags in your mouths—and you have exchanged your wedding vows before all those present today, by the powers vested in me by the State of New York, which I got free, online, I now pronounce you married. You may now kiss . . . or better yet, spank, the bride.

I think I got the tone right, no?

FEBRUARY 14

Dear Diary:

Valentine's Day!!! It just hit me. Not that I'm bitter, but I don't think it is a coincidence that the initials for Valentine's Day are VD. Perhaps I am bitter. I've only gotten two Valentines in my entire life. One from my husband, Edgar, which read, "Roses are red, violets are blue, undress one more time in front of me, and we're through!" The last was from a man I met at an AARP meeting. It was a big card that said simply, "I Pacemaker You." Years ago I faced the fact that I really have no sex appeal. Cupid saw me naked and shot an arrow into his own head.

FEBRUARY 15

Dear Diary:

I'm sad because on Valentine's Day men everywhere were buying their wives flowers and candy and jewelry in the hopes of getting a mediocre blow job (or at least a hand job with K-Y) in the laundry room later that night. And I sat all by myself, heartbroken that my vibrator didn't even have the decency to send me a card or an e-mail. I'll show it; I'm off to the supermarket today to buy a cucumber.

FEBRUARY 16

Dear Diary:

Woke up not feeling well. I spent the entire day online, on WebMD, and after eight hours of exhaustive research I've connected my symptoms to a diagnosis. And I can say with 100 percent certainty that I have pleurisy, tuberculosis, brain stem cancer or an enlarged prostate. I found a great cure for whatever ails you. God bless the Internet! A coffee enema. It worked like a charm. Not only are all my symptoms gone but I also lost twelve pounds. The only negative: I can never go back to Starbucks.

FEBRUARY 17

Dear Diary:

I'm in a post–Valentine's Day depression. Well, according to my shrink it's not really a depression—it's "appropriate sadness." Actually he's not really my shrink; he's my trainer, and I talk to him a lot when I'm on the treadmill. He's pretty smart for a steroid-riddled behemoth with huge pecs and itty-bitty nuts. Squirrels have seen him naked and said, "Pass."

FEBRUARY 18

Dear Diary:

Today is Presidents' Day, when America honors George Washington and Abraham Lincoln by offering linens half off. I think we should have a second Presidents' Day and honor JFK by offering heads half off.

FEBRUARY 19

Dear Diary:

Going on a mini tour for the next week. Giving concerts all across Canada. My agent, Shivering Steve Levine, has booked me in Toronto, Montreal, Winnipeg and Saskatoon. Steve is so proud of himself, you would have thought he'd gotten me a command performance at Buckingham Palace in front of the queen. What he actually got me is a booking in an ice bowl in Manitoba in front of a couple of old queens. I said, "Steve, thank you for booking me in Canada in the dead of winter. Any chance of getting me a week at the North Pole next January? How about a couple of days on the face of the sun in July?"

FEBRUARY 20

Dear Diary:

Driving to Toronto. No matter where I look all I see is snow. White, white, white as far as the eye can see. It's like being at Paula Deen's office party. Hundreds of miles of snow is pretty for about five minutes, then it becomes a frigid bore, like Martha Stewart.

FEBRUARY 21

Dear Diary:

Driving to Winnipeg and all I see is more snow. Boring.

FEBRUARY 22

Dear Diary:

Driving to Saskatoon. More snow. But saw a couple of people frozen to death lying like roadkill on the side of the highway. Not quite as boring.

FEBRUARY 23

Dear Diary:

The Canadian audiences I performed for were great, but I can't figure out why people live here. I think maybe they ran out of gas on their way to someplace warmer.

FEBRUARY 24

Dear Diary:

Back home from Canada. The audiences were so wonderful—they clapped until their frozen little fingers snapped off. Now I'm going to treat myself to a perfect evening—I'm going to take a bath, have Pingpong make me dinner (which I'll immediately send back), and watch TV.

Later . . . Just finished watching *Girls* on HBO. If I have to see Lena Dunham's ass, boobs or tattoos one more time, I swear to God I'm going to convene a tribunal and charge HBO with crimes against humanity. Every time Lena takes the stand it'll be like Nuremberg with cellulite. Why do homely girls insist on showing off their bodies? Who's clamoring to look at them? Even Stevie Wonder would say, "Pass." On tonight's show she wanted to show us what would be a "television first," so she hiked up her skirt, squatted and peed next to some train tracks. After seeing this I was hoping we'd see yet another "television first": Lena Dunham spraying the third rail and going up in flames. I'm glad she's "free" enough to have her fat ass on display; I just don't know why she's not free enough to have a fucking salad once in a while.

FEBRUARY 25

Dear Diary:

Off to the dentist for some major gum work. I won't be able to talk for two days. I'm despondent. Melissa couldn't be happier.

FEBRUARY 26

Dear Diary:

I have to find a new dentist. Dr. Golub did a great job; I look good *and* he saved me money (he said my face has been pulled so tight he didn't need to give me a cleaning; I can floss with the stitches behind my ears!). But he kept calling me "Joanie." Joanie! Like I'm his friend or his cousin or the local whore who gives him a hand job once a week because our mothers play cards together.

FEBRUARY 27

Dear Diary:

It's *still* Black History Month. How long do I have to keep out that picture of Martin Luther King, Jr.? And by the way, I liked him; I liked what he stood for. But what a cheaparino. He had some bucks, so why was he staying in Memphis in a $3-a-night motel? If he would've spent a little and moved into a Marriott, none of this would've happened. Sure, he could've died from a heart attack from eating in their food court (which I understand happens once a week on average), but history would have been much different.

What more can I do? And I'm starting to get pissed. Where is Ecru History Month? Naturally Pale Month? What about rosacea? Give them a week. What about vitiligo? The way I see it, they should have two months. I think *every* race, religion and ethnic group should have at least one day in their honor that's a legal holiday. And because I live in New York City, that means there would be 335 legal holidays . . . which means 335 days of suspended alternate-side-of-the-street parking . . . which means I can park anywhere I want to and all those ambulances, fire engines and emergency vehicles can go fuck themselves.

MARCH

The Jewish guy in the center kept sending everything back. "Is it vegan? Does it have peanuts in it? Is it gluten-free?" What a fuckin' whiner.

MARCH 1

Dear Diary:

Today is National Pig Day and I completely forgot to call Kevin Federline! I'll send him a note. Or a bucket of slop. He's not that fussy.

MARCH 2

Dear Diary:

I'm catching all kinds of shit because on *Fashion Police* I made one teensy little joke about Heidi Klum maybe being a Nazi. I don't know what the problem is; I was complimenting her. I said, "I haven't seen anything this hot since the Germans were pushing Jews into the ovens." You'd think I'd get a thank-you card, not just from Heidi for saying she looked nice, but from all the leftover Nazis for pointing out their ingenuity and stick-to-itiveness. But no, instead I get crap from the Anti-Defamation League for "insulting the Jews." And if I'd said "gypsies" instead of "Jews," the Jews would have been mad that I slighted them. This is why nobody likes us.

MARCH 3

Dear Diary:

I'm getting letters from people telling me I should leave Heidi Klum alone because she was "a good Nazi." What does "a good Nazi" mean? Does it mean they gave the Jews cookie dough to bake with them in the ovens? This makes me so mad that I am definitely thinking of getting a tattoo to remind people about the Holocaust. I want it to say "Six Million Plus One." The six million will be for the Jews who died in the Holocaust, and the one will be for the time I died on *Ed Sullivan*.

MARCH 4

Dear Diary:

Now I'm mad at my bank. I called to double-check that the money I'm hiding in the Cayman Islands is still hidden, and all I got was a recorded message: "If you want to check your balance, press one; if you want to transfer funds, press two . . ." How about, "If I want to kill you, I'll press your head under water for six minutes"? I hate this automated shit. If I ever did get the urge to talk to a machine I'd say "thank you" to my vibrator.

MARCH 5

Dear Diary:

Today is Multiple Personality Day and we're both so happy! Ever since *Sybil* I've been fascinated by people with multiple personality disorder. One minute you're talking to Janice from Roslyn Heights, and the next minute it's Cressida, ancient goddess of ground transportation. A couple of years ago my friend, the comedian Roseanne, announced that she had twenty-six different personalities. I was shocked. You'd think at least one of them would've gone on a diet.

I don't believe in multiple personalities; I think it's just a good way of not paying your bills. "Joan-Thrifty" would never wear $1,500 shoes. "Here, they're only a little worn, take 'em back." Yes, "Joan-Whore" slept with all those men, but "Joan-Good" would never go down on a fleet; it might bend her braces and would jeopardize her marriage to that withered, rich old man. "Joan–Child Abuse" might have taken down the horrible boy next door who continually tipped over her garbage, but "Joan-Nice" would have called the boy's parents and asked them to speak to their pastor, prior to punching little Johnny in the face, breaking his arm and leaving him sightless. (Children need to be taught boundaries.)

MARCH 6

Dear Diary:

I'm tired of dealing with crazies. When did it become my job to manage your mental illness? You wanna be nuts, be nuts. Go put a pencil in your mouth and bark at the fire hydrants, but leave me the fuck out of it.

I was leaving Citarella (where I buy day-old fish to donate to orphanages for children with clogged nasal passages) and some wacko starts following me, saying, "Jesus loves you, Jesus loves you." I said, "Look! It was just a summer thing. We were young, we were crazy, we got drunk and took a house on the Cape. Now leave me alone!"

And speaking of Christian love, I am so sick of those stupid ads for Christian singles. The ads always have some homely girl saying, "Jesus wants me to get married." I doubt this. If Jesus wanted her to get married, he would have given her a chin. I have news for you, Gloria Jean: Jesus wants you single and teaching special ed.

MARCH 7

Dear Diary:

Went to see Diana Ross in concert last night. Nine songs, a thousand costume changes and two hours of "Reach out, hold hands; sing with me, sing with me audience, sing with me . . ." Fuck off! For two hundred bucks a ticket, I'm not singing; *you* sing, you skinny bitch. How did the singing suddenly become my job? When I'm in Vegas, I don't make my audience hold hands and tell the jokes. My proctologist doesn't ask me to put my fingers up his ass.

After her show I started to go backstage to meet Diana but I just couldn't. The thought of calling anyone other than Michael Jackson "Miss Ross" depresses me so much. It's been several years and I still miss my Michael. He was such a help with my grandson, Cooper. Now that he's gone I have no one to call and tell me how to sweet-talk a young boy into doing almost anything.

Anyway, back to Big D. I remember a night way back in the '80s when Diana Ross gave a free concert in Central Park in New York. There were 200,000 people there, including me, and five minutes into the show a hurricane hit. Howling winds, driving rain—there was so much flooding it looked like Adele must've jumped into a swimming pool. People, dogs, benches were swirling by, and Diana's standing there onstage, saying, "I'll save you, I'll save you . . ." Save us? Who the fuck did she think she was, the Pope? She couldn't even save Florence Ballard, and she was a Supreme.*

---

* For those of you who don't know, Florence Ballard was one of the original Supremes. She died penniless. Would it have killed Big D to toss her a couple of shekels, or at least let her keep her dignity by sending her a sandwich? Flo could have had the choice of eating it or using it as a pillow. When you don't have much, options matter.

MARCH 8

Dear Diary:

Picked up Melissa at yoga class. They were doing the Downward-Facing Dog, but when I walked in they switched to the Downward-Facing Pig. On our way home, Melissa and I swung by a fast-food chicken place. When we got to the counter the idiot taking our order says, "We're out of breasts." I said, "Who are you? A Beverly Hills plastic surgeon a week before the Oscars?" I was livid. How is it possible that there were no breasts? Did all the chickens have mastectomies? Maybe they're roosters in drag and this is a gay chicken store and no one told the manager. If you only make one thing, there's no excuse to run out. For example, I know for a fact that if you swing by George Michael's pad, he's *never* out of butt plugs.

MARCH 9

Dear Diary:

I hate people who are lousy at their jobs. If you don't do something well, then don't do it. For example, if you weigh four hundred pounds and can't cross the street without having a triage unit on standby, don't become a personal trainer. If you stutter, don't look for work on a suicide hotline ("D-d-d-d-d-on't j-j-j-j-jump . . ." Too late). And if you give a rotten blow job, then don't become a hooker. If you can't suck a nice dick well, then find a job that doesn't require that skill, like lesbian golfer or Midwestern housewife.

MARCH 10

Dear Diary:

I've got to get caller ID. Too many people I don't know are getting through. Tonight I was lying in bed struggling with a crossword puzzle (four-letter word beginning with "c" for mean, horrible bitch; I wrote small and put in "TYRABANKS"), when the phone rang and I heard bereft sobbing.

So I listened, because at my age my friends' husbands are dropping faster than Justin Bieber's balls. And I sighed in all the right places and said "tsk-tsk" and acted like I really cared until she said, "I really be missing my Darnell." Darnell? I don't know anyone named Darnell.

From here on in, anyone who calls me better fucking identify themselves, just like they do at AA meetings. Those old winos always announce themselves. Okay, they're wrong a lot because they're drunk, but they try. "Hi, I'm the Dionne Quintuplets and I'm an alcoholic . . ." No, you're not the Dionne Quintuplets. You're a thirty-eight-year-old carpet salesman from Sheboygan named Edwin, and you have beer foam on your pants.

MARCH 11

Dear Diary:

That call about Darnell got me thinking: Names are crazy; they have no rhyme or reason. I was hoping that maybe Gwyneth Paltrow was starting a trend by naming her child after her favorite food. Her kid's name is Apple. My niece could be named Peach. And Christina Aguilera's next kid should be called Potato. I know for a fact Connie Chung's second-born is named Dog. And Kanye West's new son is going to be named Pussy in honor of where he came from.

MARCH 13

Dear Diary:

I can't stand it when an actor wins an Oscar or a Golden Globe and gets to the stage and stutters and mutters and says, "I didn't prepare anything because I didn't think I was going to win." Why the fuck didn't you prepare anything? You knew you were nominated. You had at least a 20 percent chance of winning, or 40 percent if Amy Adams was in your category. Would it have killed you to make a list of people who helped you make the movie and got you out of rehab/prison so you could make the damned thing, or your mother or your family, or your life partner, Jimmy, who makes your world go round?

I hate people who don't prepare. Who wants to walk into their accountant's office during tax season and find him shocked at having to do so much arithmetic? Or go to a proctologist and have him blurt out, horrified, "Oh, wow! Look at all the doody!"?

MARCH 16

Dear Diary:

Had lunch with my friend Brian, who's in AA, and his sponsor and his sponsor's sponsor. Ordering food took longer than the Hundred Years' War. "Is there alcohol in tiramisu?" "Does the wine burn out of the mussels?" "I could be wrong, but is there rum in the rum cake?" I'm hoping they get anorexia, so they'll starve to death and I won't have to put up with that bullshit again. And every five minutes, in the middle of a conversation, one of them would pipe in with, "Let go and let God." However, this was never said when I was reaching for the check. I wanted to get in a car and drive right into them, yelling, "Sorry! I let go and let God take the wheel."

I just want to say here that I'm thrilled with my friends' sobriety, but I'm sick and tired of hearing the competition of their rock-bottom moments. "I was drunk and raped by a gang of twelve. It was a horrible moment. Four of them were Japanese and poorly endowed." "That's nothing; I once ran nude through the White House; even Clinton booed." "That's nothing; I was so drunk I believed Richard Simmons was straight."

Sometimes I hear about celebrities who've gotten sober and I wonder what they say at their meetings. "Hi, my name is Phil Spector and I'm an alcoholic. I've kidnapped my wife, shot a woman to death and, even worse, let my hair go to hell, but I didn't drink today, so I'm a winner and I feel pretty good about myself."

"Thank you for sharing, Phillip." Clap. Clap. Clap.

MARCH 17

Dear Diary:

My friend Margie has convinced me to go to a silent retreat in the Catskill Mountains for three days. It costs almost $2,200. I said, "Margie, why not just save the money and stay home and shut the fuck up?"

MARCH 21

Dear Diary:

Thank God the retreat is over. I haven't heard that kind of silence since my wedding night when I asked Edgar, "Was it good for you?"

MARCH 23

Dear Diary:

I love Award Season. I watch all of them: the Oscars, the Grammys, the Golden Globes, etc. But I love two awards shows more than all the others: the Gay Awards

Show, which is fabulous, and the statue is an exact copy of the Oscar except it's on its knees; and the Porn Awards, which is also exactly like the Oscars except the red carpet is shaved.

MARCH 25

Dear Diary:

It's Passover and I'm at Melissa's house in L.A. for the holiday. (I'm also here for *Fashion Police*, *Joan & Melissa: Joan Knows Best?* and *In Bed with Joan*.) As much as I love Judaism, I *really* love tax write-offs. So I invited twenty-six people over, *all of whom can help me career-wise*. To me, Passover is just Thanksgiving with Jews: lots of food, lots of laughs and lots of people sending food back to the kitchen because it's too tough and you know your aunt Miriam has sensitive gums.

Very mixed guest list—Jews, Christians, atheists and homos. Should be fun. They start arriving in fifteen minutes, which gives me just enough time to do a final inspection and make sure the cater waiters have covered up their cold sores and open lesions so they don't upset my guests and ruin the four questions by adding a fifth question: "Why is there pus in my soup?"

MARCH 26

Dear Diary:

Passover dinner couldn't have gone better. It was the gayest Seder I've ever had. Two of the four questions involved Lady Gaga. When the giant lamb bone came out, half of the men at the table squealed with delight, and the other half said, "I think I know him." There's always one person at every Seder who's an uber-Jew and knows absolutely everything about Jewish history and culture and tradition. And we had ours. For the sake of kindness (and because her father's a lawyer), I'll call her Nafka. Nafka knew it all: She knew the prayers in English, Hebrew, Yiddish and Farsi; she knew the answers to all four of the questions; she even knew why Moses schlepped the Ten Commandments down the mountain instead of taking the elevator (Big M was mildly claustrophobic and had once gotten stuck for six hours in an elevator with Lot and his wife, who was not only hateful, but lived on a salt-free diet of cabbage and beans).

MARCH 27

Dear Diary:

I haven't gone to the bathroom in almost twenty-four hours. Matzoh is so binding. Now I know why it took us forty years to cross the desert.

Constipation is a terrible thing. Why do you think so many of our top serial killers (Ed Gein, Jeffrey Dahmer and John Wayne Gacy, to name a few) come from Wisconsin and its neighboring states? Cheese, that's why! Everyone knows this about cheese. I've always been surprised that those maniacs' defense lawyers didn't use this as an argument. I can just see Johnnie Cochran now: "If you eat the cheese, that revolver you'll squeeze."

I was once clogged up for a week after reaching the bottom of the Olive Garden's bottomless pasta bowl, and I was in such a foul mood that I contemplated taking out an entire Boy Scout troop right as they were practicing their knot-tying skills on their giggling gay scoutmaster.

MARCH 28

Dear Diary:

Had to run to the store to pick up milk and tampons. I buy tampons so that the teenage box-boy who works in the store will continue to look at me with both admiration and lust.

And when the fuck did milk become $8,000 a gallon? Is there a shortage? Are the cows on strike or on a work slowdown? Did Elsie and Flossie unionize, protesting work conditions? They spend all day standing in a pasture, staring at nothing and eating—just like Kevin James—so what's the problem? If I didn't care about Cooper's teeth and bones I'd cut out milk altogether and let him eat his cereal with gin or Jack, just like Grandma does.

MARCH 29

Dear Diary:

Did press all day promoting *Joan & Melissa: Joan Knows Best?* and *In Bed with Joan*. I did as many TV and radio shows in the New York tristate area as my schedule and medications would allow. All went great, although I must say I hate going on shows where the interviewer just reads the questions, regardless of what's being said. Me: "I just killed my mother." Interviewer: "I understand you like shoes?" I hate that. At least link it up with, "Did you get your mother's?"

MARCH 30

Dear Diary:

I spent all day in bed watching the Discovery ID channel. All murders, all the time; it was like the good old days on A&E when it was Hitler 24/7. (No matter how lonely or how depressed I was, I knew I could always turn to that station and get a little touch of Adolf. I was in heaven.) Nothing makes me happier than watching the police find a family of five tied up together in their rec room, bound, gagged and stiffer than Martha Stewart. My favorite episode was a cliff-hanger: All the victims were so fucking ugly that *everybody* in town had a motive to kill them. (Which begs the question: Who really was the victim here? The dead person or the townspeople who had to look at him every day?)

I got hooked on true crime when I first read Truman Capote's *In Cold Blood*, the story about two drifters in Kansas who slaughtered the Clutter family for no apparent reason. I take that back; the Clutters were simple, Christian farm folk—the drifters had a reason. I always hoped that Capote would have combined his two greatest works, *In Cold Blood* and *Breakfast at Tiffany's*, into one sequel, and the drifters wouldn't have just killed the Clutter family in that farmhouse cellar,* but they also knocked off Holly Golightly and her fucking cat, too. Now *that* book would've spent a lot of time on the bestseller list.

MARCH 31

Dear Diary:

Today is Easter. Jesus came back from the dead. I don't understand this. We're both Jews but he comes back from the dead and I can't get up before noon.

---

* Farm people have cellars where they keep tools, canned goods, camping gear and rifles. Jews have basements where we keep artwork, golf clubs and illegal kitchen help.

APRIL

According to my accountant, I spend too much. According to me, I need a new accountant.

APRIL 1

Dear Diary:

I love everybody. I think Melanie Griffith is smart smart smart smart. And John Travolta is straight as an arrow. And Jackie Chan is hung hung hung. April Fool's!

Today is April Fool's Day and I hate it because the people who play practical jokes on other people are usually assholes who think they're funny and they're not. (And to me, not being funny is a bigger sin than patricide, matricide and sometimes infanticide—but only if the baby was nice-looking.)

April Fool's Day is not a real national holiday. If it was a real holiday, Saks would be selling bedding half off, and I'd be booked at some casino or country club at a wildly inflated price.

There are a lot of different theories as to how April Fool's Day came to pass. According to Wikipedia, author/hand model Geoffrey Chaucer—who wrote *The Canterbury Tales*, the feel-good book of the fourteenth century—coined the phrase "April Fools" to refer to the engagement of Richard II to Anne of Bohemia, either because they got the date of their wedding wrong or because Anne was a taciturn, butch lesbian and Richard had no idea; he thought she was just a little frigid and a lot handy.

And as for "jokes" such as undoing the tip of a pen so it leaks or hiding cicada bugs on someone's food tray, they really aren't funny practical jokes; they're stupid. If you want to do something funny, think big. One of my favorite pranks is to run into a kindergarten class and yell out, "Little Billy? Your mommy loves your sister more than you." Wait five seconds, then run back in and say, "Just kidding! April Fool's! She actually loves your sister *and* your brother more than you!" Poor little Billy.

APRIL 3

Dear Diary:

I hate Wikipedia. There's no guarantee that what they say is true because *anyone* can go in and change the profile information. Today, I could change the part of Mother Teresa's profile that refers to her as "a humanitarian who gives assistance and aid to women and children" to "an old lezzie who dressed poorly and liked touching strangers' feet."

APRIL 5

Dear Diary:

Went out to dinner last night with one of my closest friends, whose name escapes me for the moment. Anyway, she's a diabetic and is constantly monitoring her sugar level. It was very exhausting. How many times a day can I say, "No, you're not pale and you don't look any worse than normal, but would you like to stop and get a KitKat?" She also has no boundaries, so right in the middle of dinner at Joe Allen, just as the waiter was bringing us our lump crabs, she hikes up her blouse, moves her boobs and gives herself a shot of insulin. The place went silent; it was quieter than Auschwitz the morning after shower day. She looked around at the appalled customers and said, "What? I have diabetes!" The guy at the next table said, "So what? I have colitis. You want me to take a shit in the coatroom?"

APRIL 7

Dear Diary:

I hate—not "dislike," not "am mildly annoyed by"—really hate that irritating, pasty-faced girl who plays Flo in the Progressive insurance commercials. Those commercials run during every show on every network at all hours of the day. They run so often I'm starting to miss that sexually frustrated couple that sits in separate bathtubs on the side of a cliff waiting for his hard-on medicine to kick in. Or that old couple that rides up and down the stairs endlessly on that easy-lift chair and never once seems to enjoy it and go "Wheee!"

I hate Flo. I hope she gets run over by a car . . . driven by an uninsured driver. And while she lies there waiting for an ambulance (that, God willing, is stuck in traffic), I hope the Aflac duck walks by and poops on her, just as the Geico gecko comes over and starts nibbling on her exposed, pulsating flesh.

APRIL 10

Dear Diary:

Reading the *New York Times* obituaries and I am so sad. For the fifth day in a row, not one celebrity who I'm jealous of has died. I get so annoyed reading about the untimely passing of a crossing guard, or the death of a pieceworker after a lengthy illness. These "losses" do nothing to start my day. Unless the crossing guard was run over by a school bus, or the lengthy illness was leprosy and the pieceworker died, so fittingly, piece by piece, all those obits do is waste my time and bore me half to death.

We're in desperate need of a good, tragic celebrity death. Or two. And to make it really work for me, it has to be unexpected, not like that Andy Griffith shit. Andy was three hundred fucking years old and hadn't whistled in Mayberry since 1971. I like shocking. A "Why did Whitney have cocktails in the bathtub before the Grammys?" kind of a death. A "stunning starlet and her hunky boyfriend mutual suicide pact" kind of thing, where the boyfriend "accidentally" forgot to drink the Kool-Aid and is seen "mourning" at the starlet's funeral with his arm around her best friend, who turns out to be her younger, prettier brother.

What really kills me is that with all the procedural crime shows these days, it's getting harder and harder to get away with murder. In the good old days, you shot some son of a bitch, pressed the smoking gun into his hand and you got away with it. I don't want to sound like a complainer, but nowadays, between DNA, cleaned-up blood that shows under luminol, minute crumbs from popcorn the murderer was eating six days before the crime, carpet fibers from a lesbian brothel and that nosy hag Nancy Grace who never stops prying, there's just no way a nice person like me can get away with murdering someone who really annoys me. (I personally will never forgive Nancy Grace for her treatment of Casey Anthony. Casey and her kid sat behind me on a six-hour airplane flight a week before the kid vanished. Casey had a point.)

APRIL 13

Dear Diary:

Watched Melissa McCarthy on *SNL* last night. She's hilarious. She commits to every single moment. She's more committed than Lindsay Lohan, which makes sense, since when Lindsay's committed it's usually by a court order. I hope Melissa doesn't do what a lot of stars do, and forget what made her famous. In other words, I hope she stays fat. As long as her ratings are higher than her cholesterol, who gives a shit if she smells like government cheese or has to have handlers come in twice a week to hose her down between her folds? Ruth Buzzi of *Laugh-In* decided she wanted to be pretty-ish, so she took off the hairnet and threw away the dirty sweater, and today she lives in Texas and makes a living selling nude photos of Arte Johnson on eBay. Carol Burnett went under the knife, got cheekbones and lost her series. Sonny Bono decided to "get in shape," so he took up skiing. He lost both Cher and his head. Luckily I have changed nothing. The parallel scars running up the back of my head are the result of too-tight forceps when I was delivered—as happened frequently in the fifteenth century. (And you wonder why Torquemada was always in such a bad mood?) I say, dance with the one who brung you. And in Melissa McCarthy's case, that would be Colonel Sanders and Sara Lee.

APRIL 14

Dear Diary:

I read a story in the *Times* about how John Hinckley, Jr., is behaving much more normally these days when he's out of the nut hatch, tooling about town on his day passes. I'm guessing he saw Jodie Foster's "Yup, I'm a dyke" speech on the Golden Globes and finally realized that his love for her would be unrequited. I hope he moves on with his life and from now on only obsesses about Queen Latifah, Dana Delany and Holland Taylor.

APRIL 15

Dear Diary:

Today is tax day—my favorite day of the year. Not because I like paying taxes—no one does, except for that jackass Warren Buffett, who keeps saying he wants to pay more taxes. Great, Warren, go right the fuck ahead—pay mine. My accountant's name is Michael Karlin; he'll be in touch, so have one of your five hundred servants sit by the phone.

I love tax day because I like to see fat, bald actuaries and the dumpy homely girls with bad shoes who work for them sweat like pack animals carrying supplies across the Pyrenees.

If I have to pay thousands of dollars for some lazy farmer in Kansas to not grow corn, or for some teenage mother in Houston to feed her five kids by seven different baby daddies, then I want somebody to be as miserable as I am when I write the checks. I want to share the pain. Why? Because I'm a giver.

APRIL 16

Dear Diary:

Today is the day after taxes were due and I'm feeling very poor. So I decided to go out and treat myself to lunch at the Olive Garden and lose myself in their bottomless pasta bowl. And so I did. At lunch today, when I asked the waiter for coffee, he said, "No problem."

What does he mean, "no problem"? If I had asked for decaf would it have been a problem? Would green tea have been an issue? If I ordered a latte would he have considered it an international crisis requiring emergency aid from FEMA, the Red Cross and a couple of recently molested Boy Scouts doing good deeds in an effort to wash away the trauma?

APRIL 17

Dear Diary:

There are a lot of *other* expressions along with "no problem" that I hate:

GOOD JOB: I hate it when a parent tells a toddler "good job" after the little moron makes potty in the toilet instead of his diaper. It's not a job; it's nature. Little Billy's not on your payroll; he's not getting a matching 401(k) contribution; he's not invested in a confusing, mediocre pension plan. He's two, and potty training is the *parents'* job, not his. When my dementia-riddled ninety-six-year-old aunt Sadie takes a shit in the toilet instead of the sink, *that's* a good job. And if you don't believe me, ask her caregiver, who has OCD and washes her hands six hundred times a day. And now that we're talking about potty training, what's wrong with this picture? It takes years for a kid to learn the simple task of elimination (which I feel is one of nature's few mistakes) and we're applauding? Homo sapiens are supposed to be the smartest ones on the planet; how come it takes the dogs three weeks—I repeat, *three weeks*—to get the hang of it, and Junior is walking around with a load in his pants on his way to geometry class?

GIVE ME THE 411: If you want information from somebody, just do what everybody else does: Say, "What do you know about that?" Or do what every black person does: Say, "Let me ax you somethin'." But don't say, "Give me the 411." It's not cute. It's stupid. It's like visiting a hospital ward filled with terminal cancer patients and saying, "Who's on the clock?"

. . . **NOT:** I hate it when people say, "I like her . . . NOT." I hope people who say that get hit by a car, and then I can go to the hospital and keep them on life support . . . NOT.

MY BAD: Just because you're admitting you made a mistake doesn't make it okay. "My bad" is not an excuse or a defense. I have taken the time to trace the origin of it. It started at the Nuremberg Trials when Adolf Eichmann, who sat shackled in his bulletproof-glass booth, was asked by the prosecuting attorney, "Sir, is it not true that you alone are responsible for the cold-blooded gassing of six million Jews?" He replied, "Mein bad."

HAVE A GOOD ONE: Have a good one what? What the fuck are they talking about? Be specific! Bowel movement? Bank heist? Three-way with my cousin Charlotte? When someone says, "Have a good one," I assume they mean "day," but how lazy do you have to be that you can't finish the sentence without becoming exhausted? "One" and "day" have the same number of letters, so why switch them at all? It's not like they're replacing "colostomy" or "terrorist uprising." And if you're in that kind of rush, then close your piehole and move on and don't talk at all. If it's an emergency, just scream and point and jump up and down and I'll get the message. That's what Gandhi did.

HOOKING UP: Teenagers who have casual random sex refer to these magical moments as "hooking up." This doesn't sound romantic; it sounds like you've got a boat tied to the back of your Jeep and you're dragging it down the freeway. Or, another way to put it, like you're butt-humping Carnie Wilson.

APRIL 18

Dear Diary:

Speaking of butt-humping, my friend Larry brought over a bootleg copy of *Behind the Candelabra*, and we watched it in my den under a blanket. It's the HBO movie about Liberace and his boy toy, Scott Thorson. It was touching and sad and the sex scene was so sweet. The sight of a sixty-eight-year-old Polish immigrant getting drilled through the headboard by an underage street urchin brought a tear to my eye. This is what makes America great.

Michael Douglas, who plays Liberace, and Matt Damon, who plays his boyfriend, Scott (maybe just a bit too convincingly as a homo), are in bed having just finished a marathon fuck-fest and Scott, who is supposed to be sixteen, asks Liberace how he managed to stay hard all night long. And Liberace tells him he's had penile implants. I don't know if that means his junk will rust during a blow job, but I was quite impressed.

Implants just take the worry out of sex. If only I could have had something comparable, like a drawstring on my vagina. My marriage would have been so much happier. "Wanna little nookie, Edgar?" I'd just pull it tight. Time to pop out Melissa? I'd loosen it up! I wish I had known God when he was creating us (I was born two years later)—I don't think the man was paying attention. Maybe he was preoccupied watching Gwyneth Paltrow jamming a gluten-free cupcake into her skeletal frame and thinking, "My bad."

APRIL 20

Dear Diary:

Tonight I watched *Game of Thrones* on TV. I'm tired of hearing what a great actor Peter Dinklage is. "He's so good you don't even know he's a dwarf!" I don't even know he's on the show half the time 'cause he's below the frame in medium shots. And in the long shots when they dress him in dark colors I often mistake him for a tree stump or a large family pet.

You definitely know Peter's a dwarf. I saw him in *The Sound of Music*. He's one-third the size of the smallest von Trapp child. When Maria sang "Climb Every Mountain," he begged for a Sherpa to help him hike across the lip of the stage. I read an interview with Peter where he said that as a dwarf he would never demean himself by playing a Christmas elf. Hey, Tiny, here's a newsflash—you're the only famous dwarf in Hollywood. Whatever part you want, you get. When there's a casting call for a dwarf, your name's the only one on the sign-up sheet. What are you, crazy? I'd play a mean, humpbacked old Jew in a second if they asked, except that Christian bitch Jane Fonda always gets those roles. Your fellow dwarves would be happy to work at the North Pole, so get off your self-righteous booster chair and have a moment of gratitude. Although I must admit he is a fabulous actor.

APRIL 21

Dear Diary:

And while we're at it, why are there no dwarves on *The Walking Dead*? Are there no zombie dwarves? Something is very wrong. Why is it that when they all come tumbling toward me, bloody as shit, they're all five-foot-eight and over?

I also started wondering if dwarves are well hung. Midgets are probably not because everything about them is in proportion—it's all the same size, all small.

Dwarves are another case. They have little arms and legs, but sturdy torsos and massive heads. They must fit into the bell curve like the rest of humanity—some are well hung, some are not, and I'm sure that Japanese dwarves look like Brillo pads with buttons. A lot of dwarves are very virile, case in point, the late great Michael Dunn, who said to Tina Louise, "If you've never been with a dwarf, get ready, because I am going to make the most passionate, wildest, craziest love to you." And she said, "If you do and I find out, I'm going to be very upset."

APRIL 22

Dear Diary:

When I'm stressed I do one of two things: I draw a warm bath, get in, take my teeth out, put on Eminem's "The Real Slim Shady" and just drift. Or I watch old movies for comfort. Today I chose the latter and went to bed early and watched *Children of a Lesser God* on Turner Classic Movies. I'd forgotten how moving it was. And I'd forgotten that Marlee Matlin won the Oscar for Best Actress. And I'd forgotten that I couldn't understand one word she said. Even last night, the second time around, I couldn't figure it out. She's moaning, she's grimacing, she's signing . . . I didn't know if she was an actress in a role or a gangbanger having an orgasm.

APRIL 23

Dear Diary:

Last night while trying to find the Sex Toy Channel, which was featuring Japanese rabia tickrers, I watched the news. Some athlete was being interviewed after a game and he said he was "FUstrated" at his team's losing. What's with the "FUstrated"? What happened to the *r*? It's not silent. The word is "FRustrated," not "FUstrated." That sort of stupidity drives me cazy.

Also, I hate it when people drop the *g* at the end of a word. "He was runnin' and playin' and singin' . . ." Again, the *g* is not a silent letter. Letters are meant to be used. And where will it end? How would you like it if I walked into Red Lobster and ordered an Angus burger, but I didn't pronounce the *g*?

APRIL 24

Dear Diary:

Couldn't concentrate on anything today. I kept thinking maybe we should just start all over and change the rules of spelling and pronunciation. For example, if we changed the first letter on a lot of words, we'd never have to worry about political correctness again. Example: I wouldn't be upset if Mel Gibson called me a dike. And Paula Deen surely would be back in business if she said, "I hate Tiggers, don't you?" Just by changing one letter, making "gook" into "kook," Ann Curry would have laughed her tight little laugh when Matt Lauer said, "Here comes that dog-munching kook." And I would not be upset when Father Desmond Tutu called me a punt. This could be the end of hatred, worldwide! If Nelson Mandela was alive I would say, "Somebody get me that old toon on the phone. Tell him it's the Newish Witch."

APRIL 25

Dear Diary:

I hate the autocorrect on my computer, phone and iPad. It's humorless and doesn't understand nuance; it's the Jay Leno of apps. Today I was writing a pretty little poem called "I Hope You Die," about all of the skinny bitches in Hollywood—okay, it was more of an homage to eating disorders—and I wrote that one starlet, who shall remain nameless (and FYI, it's *not* Ashley Olsen), looked a little "AIDS-y."

The autocorrect kept changing "AIDS-y" to "antsy" or "artsy." This starlet doesn't look nervous or creative; she looks like she has six T cells. I know what I meant; autocorrect doesn't. So let's lose that "tool," shall we? I spent a hundred grand on a degree in linguistics; I don't need a phone app telling me what to do with my colon.

Although in fairness, the autocorrect isn't always wrong. Every time you type the name "Joan Rivers," autocorrect changes it to "Insufferable Cunt."

APRIL 26

Dear Diary:

Some day! Sat down on my sunny terrace to enjoy a nice latte and answer my hate mail, which has been piling up since last Valentine's Day. (Good news is, my house is under consideration to be on *Hoarders*.) My neighbor Leah came over here hysterical because she found out her husband, Murray, has been cheating on her. I felt sorry for her, not because he was cheating but because she's a dope; *everyone* knew he was cheating. Friends, coworkers, doormen knew; a blind passerby could figure it out in two seconds. But not Leah. I said to her sweetly, "Leah, you fucking moron, what kind of an asshole idiot are you? How did you not know? For openers, Murray has teeth marks on his dick and you wear a denture. Second, half the kids in the neighborhood have his nose. And third, when you go to a Yankees game and thirty thousand fans yell out, 'Hi, Dad!' aren't you a little suspicious? And let's not forget the time I got into a taxi and said to the driver, 'Where can a girl get a little action in this town?' and he took me to Murray's office."

I can't stand stupid. Jennifer Aniston has dated, been cheated on and dumped by almost every man west of

Phoenix and yet she's always shocked when the shit hits the fan. And what about that psychotic bitch Mia Farrow? When she found out that Woody Allen was schtupping her daughter Soon-Yi, she said she was stunned. Never saw it coming. How is that possible? Not three days earlier Mia caught him jerking off to *Flower Drum Song*. He wore soy sauce as cologne. He'd go to the zoo and stare lovingly at the giant pandas Ching Ching and Ling Ling.

APRIL 27

Dear Diary:

The dumb parade continues. I went to the bookstore to buy the Jewish version of *Fifty Shades of Grey*, *Thirty-Three Shades of Grey* (we always get a third off), and the guy at the Help Desk was helpless. I asked him if my favorite author, Ann Rule, had any new books coming out. I said, "True crime." He said, "Is that the title?" I said, "No, the genre." He stared. So I said, "Category," and he went on the computer to look. I then asked him if they had Paul Anka's new autobiography. He said, "Who's the author?" I said, "Mark Twain." He said, "Is it new?" I explained who Mark Twain was and he said, "Well, how should I know that? It was before my time." I said, "The Stone Age is before my time, but I've heard of it." He said, "Cool."

APRIL 28

Dear Diary:

Damn, I was woken up today at 6:50 a.m., and it's my day off. Why? Because the gardener, Jose, that adorable wetback who's in this country illegally, thought that would be a good time for mowing and blowing. I don't get it. Even John Travolta doesn't start blowing until noon.

I love illegals, mainly because they can't complain. Who are they going to complain to? Having illegals is as close to slavery as we can get in this country since Abe "Boy Did I Make a Mistake" Lincoln messed it up for all of us. Okay, fine, I agree: Slavery was totally wrong for the African-Americans, but why shelve a great program because it didn't work for one group? Believe me, there are a lot of Kazakhstanis who would love a free trip to this country in accommodations similar to the Carnival cruise ship the *Commode of the Sea*. And when they land here they'll have a warm bed in a perfectly nice closet and three delicious meals of leftovers a day in exchange for twenty hours of labor. (Yes, twenty hours—it takes time to really brush down a vintage Chanel suede cape.)

APRIL 29

Dear Diary:

Thought for the day: Words of kindness are wildly overrated. Someone today in the Piggly Wiggly said, "Let this old lady go first. She looks like she's fading." Everyone moved and let me through and I thought, "Too easy, Jell-O heads. Kind words are cheap; if you want to be nice to me, pay for my fucking groceries." You can tell me I'm a piece of human garbage, a complete waste of good skin, one of God's worst efforts, and as long as your check clears, you and I are pals. I'm thinking of doing a needlepoint on this. I already have a pillow that says, "Don't expect praise without envy until you are dead." I keep it on the bed in my guest room, right next to the pillow that says, "Don't sit on my face if you have dandruff."

MAY

You know what they say:
"Once you go Jew, there's no other screw!"

MAY 1

Dear Diary:

Today is May Day and we're supposed to celebrate it by dancing around a Maypole. I've never actually seen a Maypole, let alone people who danced around one. The closest thing like that I've ever seen was a group of soccer fans surrounding Victoria Beckham, marveling that she had the strength to stand up.

MAY 2

Dear Diary:

Saw Sally Field on TV tonight selling Boniva, the pill for osteoporosis. This is a commercial I not only wanted but would have been so right for, as my bones snap so often people think I'm doing a commercial for peanut brittle. Sally says, "I'm too busy to take a pill every day, but with Boniva I only have to take one pill a month." Too busy? Doing what? Pulling a baby out of a pit bull's mouth? Sitting at the table with Israel and Palestine trying to negotiate peace? The woman makes one movie every nine years. Big Sal's got nothing *but* time on her hands. When did she become so fucking busy? I—who am actually busy—took time off to figure out how long it takes me to take a pill. Two minutes, tops, including getting a glass of water. What has Sally Field got to do that's so important besides making her daily call to her agent—collect—sobbing and begging for work? I think Sally should stop taking Boniva and just let her bones break. Then she could get an endorsement deal for Rice Krispies, pull in a *much* younger demo and inspire a new generation of fans who'll like her, really, really like her. I should call Sally and tell her. But the bitch probably doesn't have the time to pick up the phone.

MAY 3

Dear Diary:

I read a story in some rag today (the *New York Times*) about Chaz Bono, who is still talking about her sex change. Chaz says she "identifies as a man." Excuse me, Chaz, you still have a vagina. Hold a mirror between your knees and point it up! I don't care if she lopped off her tits with a Garden Weasel and has mats of hair plus a battleship tattoo on her chest; if she has a vagina, she's still a woman. What if I decided to identify as a coffee table? Even if I have my legs polished and put a lamp on my head, technically, if I have a vagina, I'd still be a woman. And why give it up? When was the last time a man pulled out a chair for a coffee table? If you want to add a penis, fine, but if you're any kind of an athlete, don't give up your vagina. Figure it out! If you're a runner, how fabulous is it to have a rainproof inside pocket? You can keep your hands free and still be able to have your phone, your mints and even a Kleenex, or if you're Octomom, a nightstand, a skateboard and a Honda Accord to drive home from the meet in. Also, if you give up your vagina, think of all the pet names you can no longer use for it: Hooha, Vajayjay, Daddy's Little Clam, Momma's Twitchy Friend, Whisker Biscuit, South Mouth, and if you're in the cast of *Duck Dynasty*—Uncle's Best Girl.

MAY 4

Dear Diary:

I saw some old musical show on TV last night and I must confess: I *still* don't get David Bowie. Since he first broke onto the scene in the '70s, I've tried to figure him out but couldn't. Even his gorgeous wife, Iman, crosses her eyes and makes faces behind his back. In the '70s, I wanted people to think I was hip so I pretended to get him. I'd act like I knew what the fuck Ziggy Stardust was all about and only called him Bowie—cool people just called him Bowie. He was like the Bono or Cher of his day except he could actually sing, and even if he couldn't he was a seminal influence on the music. You want a seminal influence? Talk to Madonna; she considers it a food group. I can't figure out if David Bowie is straight, gay, bisexual, trisexual, quadrisexual or maybe just a Minotaur. Elton John I got right from the get-go. He could sing, he could write, he could suck a dick. You always knew where he stood. Or knelt. And I still get Elton today, now that he's a cutie-pie, rich old queen with a husband, a family, a castle and a bunch of wig-lets. But Bowie, even with that stunning, bulimic African supermodel wife . . . not a clue.

MAY 5

Dear Diary:

My birthday is coming up next month and I think Melissa and Cooper are planning a big surprise party because they keep looking at me and then whispering to each other, "How much longer? When is it going to happen already? It's time, I'm telling you, it's time."

I know they care about me and my quality of life because when I complained about having a bad hair day over the weekend, Melissa went to court to fight for my right to die.

MAY 6

Dear Diary:

I was watching some TV newsmagazine tonight and they did a story on prostitution that infuriated me. They were against it. In today's tough economic climate, I find that unconscionable. Why would some self-righteous, Manolo-wearing "journalist" begrudge a gal for trying to pay the rent by giving hummers to tire salesmen in an alley, behind a Dumpster? (1) Who's she bothering? (2) In kneepads and mouthwash alone, she's putting plenty of money back into the economy. (3) There are a lot of tire salesmen who won't be so stressed out that they ruin their lives by turning to drink.

The report said prostitutes were nothing more than sad, lonely women who had bad sex with unattractive bald men in exchange for money, jewelry or rent. They sound exactly like housewives to me, except they don't have to take care of his pasty, fat children from his first marriage to the woman who supported him when he went to college.

MAY 7

Dear Diary:

I saw the Broadway show *Annie* tonight. It was cheerful, and if there's one thing I hate, it's cheerful musicals. Bo-ring. *Annie* would have been a lot better if Miss Hannigan, the head of the orphanage, killed at least one of the ethnic kids, or Daddy Warbucks was brought up on child molestation charges.

MAY 8

Dear Diary:

Flew back to L.A. to film episodes of *Joan & Melissa: Joan Knows Best?* I love having a reality show. I feel like one of the Kardashian girls except I don't have a sex tape or back hair.

Speaking of sex tapes . . . one of the story lines on *JKB* this season is that I made a parody sex tape with Ray J. The scene came out very funny and Ray J was great to work with—he's really smart and very sweet. If Ray J and I ever really made a sex tape, we decided the possible names could be:

Dry Hard
On Golden Shower
I Am Curious (Brown)
Last Bingo in Paris
Pile-Driving Miss Daisy
Brown and Out in Beverly Hills
or
To Drill a Mockingbird

MAY 9

Dear Diary:

Had a moment in the supermarket today. I told Melissa I'd pick up dinner tonight, so on my way home from the studio I stopped in at Ralphs to buy some food. As I'm checking out, the cashier says, "Paper or plastic? And remember, due to L.A. laws, next year there will be no more plastic bags and paper bags will be twenty-five cents apiece." She said it's because they're trying to conserve trees. Bullshit. Someone's making a profit. If you really want to conserve trees, make us all become

Muslims and, instead of using toilet paper, we'll wipe our asses with our left hands.

I went nuts. I held up the entire checkout line and demanded to speak to Ralph. "What do you mean we have to pay for the bag? If we refuse, how are we supposed to get all the food home? Eat it right here on the counter, like Mama Cass did?" A supermarket not having shopping bags is like a restaurant not having plates. What do they do, just have the chef throw the food in your mouth? It's like the proctologist who makes you pay extra to have the hose pulled out of your ass. Some things should just be free, like shopping bags in the supermarket or VD tests after a date with John Mayer.

MAY 10

Dear Diary:

I've had it with Facebook. I woke up this morning and I had sixty-three "pokes." I may not have much feeling down there anymore, but if I'm poked sixty-three times I'm pretty sure I'd notice either a tickle, a trickle or some mild chafing.

I'm tired of having my computer clogged up with messages from idiots with nothing to say. "Norma is at the Laundromat fluffing her whites." "Jesse B. likes Denny's blueberry waffles." "Tim is at the Coffee Bean with Aaron and he's having an espresso." The only way I'd care if Tim was at the Coffee Bean would be if he was there with a locked and loaded AK-47 and was having an episode. If Tim opened fire on the bunch of pretentious assholes who were sipping their Double Venti Chai Green Teas, then, and only then, would it be worth my time to read angry Timmy's post.

MAY 11

Dear Diary:

Got rid of Facebook today and I feel as free as the woman in the tampon commercial who can go swimming, surfing or cliff diving in spite of her heavy flow.

MAY 12

Dear Diary:

Reread my entry from the other day and I realized I made a mistake—maniacs with AK-47s don't go into Coffee Beans; they go into schools, which is an ugly phenomenon I really don't understand. My third-grade teacher, Mrs. Gotbaum, was a malevolent cunt, but it never dawned on me to pull an Uzi out of my purse and mow down the entire cafeteria. I was perfectly happy just urinating on the apples I left on her desk every day.

If these crazies feel the need to gun down strangers, might I suggest they leave schools alone and reroute themselves to local nursing homes or assisted-living facilities? I don't mean to be callous (if Melissa had her way I'd have been in Shady Pines years ago), but all those whiny widows are waiting for the white light anyway, so why prolong their damp diapers and clicking dentures? No one likes a long good-bye. This would also be good for their families because it not only saves money, but it takes away the stress of playing "Who's Going to Smother Grandma?"

MAY 13

Dear Diary:

Took my darling thirteen-year-old grandson, Cooper, for a haircut today and the stylist kept asking him if he wanted some "product" in his hair. What the fuck is "product"? If it's gel, call it gel. "Product" could be anything—liverwurst, chocolate pudding, uranium . . . Beauticians need to be more specific. When I go out for dinner, I don't order "mammal" or "aquatic vertebrate." I order a porterhouse steak or Flipper au gratin. When I go shopping at Bergdorf, I don't say, "Gimme cloth." I say, "I'd like a couture Dior gown, black with gold trim, sewn together by an old-before-her-time Colombian peasant woman named Carmela."

When we left the salon I paid in "product." I gently placed my gum in his hand. Mick Jagger's brings in fifty bucks on eBay.

MAY 14

Dear Diary:

Took the red-eye back to New York last night as we have a co-op board meeting today. We're hiring a new doorman. Everyone in the building had some specific thing they wanted. I wanted someone who can keep a fucking secret as to who comes in and out of my apartment. I'm lobbying hard for Marlee Matlin. The woman in #13B wanted someone very tall and imposing who would understand that being a doorman is a service job and would be required to service her twice a week whether he wants to or not, even when she keeps her braces on her legs. The gal in #12G wanted someone who speaks at least three languages, as she works for the UN in human trafficking and has taken her girls out of a horrific life and now runs a lucrative business, Maids Without Passports.

MAY 15

Dear Diary:

I can't believe it. In only twenty-four hours we hired a doorman and nearly everyone in the building is happy. (Except for Alan Alzheimer's in #12F who thinks he's in Hawaii and is demanding hula girls and leis every time he comes downstairs.) We hired a six-foot-seven behemoth who can speak nine languages fluently, none of them English!

MAY 16

Dear Diary:

It was all over the news that Angelina Jolie had a double mastectomy to prevent getting cancer. What a role model Angie is. How courageous! I think Paris Hilton should take a page from Angie's book and step up to the plate and try to prevent STDs. It would be so easy for her. All she would have to do is have her knees fused together. I would be glad to write the first check for a welder's mask.

MAY 17

Dear Diary:

There's a new commercial on television that's really annoying the shit out of me. It's a military recruiting ad and it says, "Are you strong or Army strong?" Not to diminish our soldiers, because "Army strong" is good, but it's not the benchmark for strength. Broccoli farts are. C'mon, face it, what do you think will clear out a cave full of terrorists faster: ten well-trained soldiers or one old man with an explosive lower intestine? I rest my case. Broccoli-fart strong trumps Army strong, every time.

MAY 19

Dear Diary:

Watched a Discovery Channel special on squirrels tonight. Fascinating. Who knew they were good for anything but sprucing up an old jacket with collars and cuffs? For example, the average squirrel can keep nuts in his mouth for months on end and everyone's impressed. And yet, when poor Clay Aiken does it, everyone's nauseous.

MAY 20

Dear Diary:

I don't know why but I woke up this morning feeling depressed. Maybe because it was raining and dreary, or maybe it's because I've gained five pounds, or maybe if I really want to look into my heart, it's because Betty White's career is doing so much better than mine. Whatever. None of my usual pick-me-ups worked (shopping, berating staff, giving orphans the finger), so I tried something new. I put on my finest Chanel suit, grabbed my best jewelry, stuffed my purse with cash, went down to Skid Row and rolled my eyes at the homeless. In less than an hour—actually, forty minutes (remember, I'm Jewish so, as I said before, I always take a third off)—I felt better about myself and limoed over to Tiffany's to buy me a little "you did good, Joan" diamond bauble. I tried the same "I want a third off" shtick in Tiffany's but they wouldn't buy it. Anti-Semitic bastards. (I'll bet somewhere in the basement, i.e., bunker, they have drawers of diamond-studded swastikas they only show to tall, blond, blue-eyed Aryans.)

MAY 21

Dear Diary:

I hate the spring. One day it's cool and lovely, the next day it's cold and blustery, and the day after that it's a million degrees and humid. Today was muggy. It was so muggy I was sweating like R. Kelly at a Girl Scout Jamboree. I went through two pairs of pants, three Spanx and the Depends I keep in my purse for "special occasions." I decided to stay only in air-conditioned places, so I went to the Museum of Modern Art and looked at the pictures. To amuse myself I bought a bag of M&M's, which I spit all over the Jackson Pollocks and nobody noticed.

MAY 22

Dear Diary:

On my flight back from L.A., I wound up sitting next to a Holocaust survivor. We exchanged stories about the camps. She told me about how at Auschwitz she had no food and no hot water and she never knew if she was going to live or die. I told her about how at Camp Kinnekineck in Connecticut I had no makeup and no jewelry and I never knew if I was going to have a boyfriend or not. We commiserated with each other and then decided that even if our lives sucked, at least we weren't desperate losers like those needy whores on *The Bachelor.*

MAY 23

Dear Diary:

I'm back in L.A. for a "minor cosmetic procedure." I'm having a brow lift, tummy tuck, chin job and lip implant—or as my plastic surgeon likes to call it, "the usual." Should be all healed in forty-eight hours. If not I'll just tell people I spent a romantic weekend with Chris Brown.

MAY 24

Dear Diary:

My agent, Self-righteous Steve Levine, called and asked me if I wanted to do a PSA for child abuse. I asked him how much, and then said, "Great, no problem. Will I be for it or against it?"

MAY 25

Dear Diary:

It's the day before Memorial Day weekend starts and wow, my bandages are off! Although my face is totally lopsided and puffy and I look haggard and hungover from the anesthetic, several fans kept asking for my autograph. I signed, "Much love, Sharon Stone." Off to the store for a few last-minute purchases. I don't know which colors will go with my bruises and scars, but he may have pulled a bit too much this time; I find I am talking through my part and shitting through my ears.

MAY 27

Dear Diary:

I normally don't write in the morning but the day started with such a jolt I feel compelled. Today is Memorial Day. I love this holiday mainly because it's the easiest holiday to dress correctly for. I don't have to do anything. I simply emphasize my pasty white old lady legs by wearing short shorts, and then add a touch of red with my red spider veins and a smidgen of blue with my big varicose numbers. It's great! I can just fall out of bed and be ready to march with the Old Veteran Geezers. If I sit on a float and kick my legs fast enough they'll think it's a flag.

Just had my coffee and Restylane and I opened the paper and what do I see? There, on the front page, is a picture of the Pope . . . in his *red* outfit. And on Memorial Day! And you wonder why people are leaving the Church. Pedophilia's one thing, but there's no excuse for bad fashion. The man spends half the year wearing white out of season and then, on the *first day* he's allowed to wear white, *should* wear white, he's in a scarlet gown with matching tam and slippers. I'd say, "There is no God," but I believe there is. I just believe he either doesn't have any fashion sense or he has his priorities fucked up, and he's mistakenly more interested in saving children than in dressing for the season.

I love the new Pope, Francis. I was there when they were naming him. I was worried because the man is not an American and I was scared some jokester cardinal would opt for the name Sandusky. I should cut the Pope a little slack; he's new at Poping, and with the old Pope hanging around the Vatican looking over his shoulder, counting the jewelry, maybe he's too nervous to pay attention to detail. A lot of people don't realize how hard it is to be a Pope. It's not all just good times and wearing fabulous rings and waving to no one in particular. So I made a list of potential papal troubles:

1. Those snappy hats cause baldness.
2. There are no pockets in the vestments. Where does he keep his Altoids? No one needs a pontiff with altar boy on his breath.
3. He always makes the sign of the cross with his right arm, which means the left one has no muscle tone and it just lies there doing

nothing, like Katie Holmes's vagina on her wedding night.

4. He's constantly saying "bless you" to people. What does he say when somebody sneezes? "Bless you, bless you"? He can't say, "Jesus Christ, you got snot on my scepter!"

MAY 28

Dear Diary:

Just got back from doing a benefit for U.S. war veterans and I'm exhausted. Once a year I try to entertain our wounded warriors, but frankly I feel the government is inflating the numbers a bit. I know all about Photoshopping. It's like Princess Diana walking through the land mines. Yeah, right. I knew her. The only time that bitch left Kensington Palace was to bang her Arab boyfriends in the back of their cars. If she was really walking through mines, how come she never got blown up? It's not like she was so careful; she wore heels. Diana was never in peril and died as an oversexed, drug-addled princess should—decently, in a tunnel in Paris.

I spent forty-five minutes at the Old Soldiers' Home trying to explain *RuPaul's Drag Race* to a bunch of shaky old men who suffer from post-traumatic stress disorder. All of them spent the entire show hiding under their wheelchairs because my voice reminded them of the Vietcong Tabernacle Choir.

Seriously, I truly believe Memorial Day is important. It reminds me of how great America is, and that it's well worth putting other people's lives on the line to protect and defend it. If it weren't for America, Mexicans would have to tunnel to Japan to find day labor picking fruit or trimming hedges or saying "You finish?" to customers in restaurants who appear to be in no way done with their meals. (How often I want to say to these guys, "Back up, Jose, I'm not even chewing yet.")

MAY 29

Dear Diary:

I did something I've never done before because of Memorial Day weekend. I bought a mattress and box spring half off. I love holiday sales because nothing reminds me of what Memorial Day truly stands for like a mattress sale. I didn't really need a mattress, but the opportunity to get a nice nap in was too good to pass up. I laid right down in the store and lulled myself to sleep with thoughts of how the gooks tortured and brainwashed our boys. Besides, how could I miss the chance to get a big-ticket item at 50 percent off *and* leave DNA samples on a store full of mattresses for strangers to roll around in? One more thing I can cross off my bucket list.

MAY 30

Dear Diary:

Flew into Las Vegas tonight to do a show and our plane was two hours late because some fatso—in coach, mind you—collapsed from an "irregular heartbeat." Blimpy doubled over and seized when the flight attendant told him they'd run out of sandwiches. And because of this we had to make an emergency landing in Ontario, which really pissed me off because there's no good shopping there and I don't bowl. The paramedics came aboard and tried to revive Chunky Charlie. Nothing worked. He was turning blue and swelling and actually starting to get that telltale "I'm dead and you're not" odor, until I suggested putting a brisket under his nose. This always works very well in my family. This is a very good story: Tanta Rose literally had the formaldehyde needle in her ass when she smelled the undertaker's meatball sandwich. She sat up and lived for another twenty years, kinehora. The same happened with Chubbo and we were soon back on our way.

I love Las Vegas, all the glitz, the glamour, the great shows, but I'd forgotten how stupid showgirls are. And I swear to God they've gotten even stupider. In the old days they were so dumb you'd stump them by asking, "Quick! Spell MGM backwards." And they couldn't. Now they can't even spell O. Magicians are still all over the place and I'm glad. I have always loved magicians. My first job after college was working as an assistant for Kuda Bux. He was more than a magician. Rumor has it that in India he had been a gynecologist. I believe this because his finale trick was to pull a hat out of a rabbit.

But even the plain magicians aren't what they used to be. They used to do a couple of card tricks, bend a spoon or saw a person in half. (Jeffrey Dahmer closed with that theatrical feat, didn't he?) Nowadays their tricks are so huge, many of them don't even fit into showrooms. David Copperfield carried on and got huge applause because he made the Statue of Liberty "disappear." Big fuckin' deal—Mohamed Atta made the Twin Towers disappear and not only did he not milk it for applause, he didn't even have a cape.

The granddaddies of magic of course were Siegfried and Roy. I ran into Siegfried today. Actually I didn't run into him, I tripped over him. He was sitting on a curb mumbling to himself the words to "Deutschland über Alles." Ever since their act broke up when Roy got mauled by a tiger, Siegfried has been a shadow of his former magical self. I was coming out of a restaurant in the hotel, having eaten the delicious Wayne Newton sandwich—ham on fat bread—and there was Siegfried, cracking a threadbare whip and meowing mournfully. He started crying and singing "Edelweiss," so I slipped him a couple of bucks, and I walked away. And as I left I heard him say, "Five dollars?!?! Who am I, Lance Burton? Do you know who I am? We were the first. We were the first to make lions sit; we were the first to make tigers beg. We were the first to have anal sex onstage—and not just with each other, but with our favorite snow leopard, Cindy. And you give me five dollars?" He was totally right. I felt so guilty I went back and dropped another fiver in his hat and said, "Buy something nice for Cindy and the kids."

MAY 31

Dear Diary:

Got to thinking: What kind of a fucking idiot was Roy to get mauled the way he did? Even a fearless immigrant like Roy should have known he was looking for trouble. You unlock the cage of a huge tiger and let him run free and then act all pissy when he tries to eat you? The mauling was Roy's own fault. (1) He and Siegfried should have fed the tiger before the show. (2) He and Siegfried should not have worn shiny sequins. (3) He and Siegfried should *never* have used butter as a lube.

JUNE

When I popped out of the cake, there was no shadow. Hooray! Six more weeks of nagging!

JUNE 1

Dear Diary:

My birthday—ugh—is around the corner and all I keep thinking about is where and how they will find my body when I die. Since I've achieved some fame (I'm being modest here because you paid for this book and I don't want you to hate me), when I go, probably—if it's a slow news day—it will be in all the papers and on TV (that cute little Selena Gomez ought to thank her lucky stars she won't have to worry about that), which means I'll have to produce the event so that it is not only newsworthy but will set Melissa and Cooper up for a ninety-minute HBO special on their grief and/or happiness at my passing.

Since I'm old there won't be any "she died so young" beats to play, and since I don't have any major drug or alcohol addictions we can't use the "I'm surprised she lived this long" card. Which leaves either natural causes or freak accidents. Cancer, heart attack and stroke are boring, and at my age . . . uh . . . uh . . . uh . . . you know the thing where you forget . . . oh yeah . . . Alzheimer's is not unexpected. The only way Alzheimer's becomes interesting is if it causes someone to take a bath with the toaster or mistake a wood chipper for a Jacuzzi.

Because of the birthday I've been thinking a lot about my funeral. Death does not scare me. My father was a doctor so I saw death often—mainly because he was not a very good doctor. I think funerals should be memorable. For example, I went to a beautiful gay funeral for my gay neighbor who died after having a heart attack while trying to get to his stress management class on time. It was so elegant; all the men were dressed in black and pearls and they had his body, in honor of his homosexuality, lying on his stomach. The only negative thing was the poor choice of music. Instead of Mozart's Requiem Mass in D Minor, his husband chose something he thought would be more relevant: "Don't Get Around Much Anymore." So I thought of making a list of what Melissa should and should not do at my funeral:

- Make sure the guy who cuts the tombstone is a good speller.
- Don't break the news to my friends by singing, "A-Tisket, A-Tasket, Joan's Finally in a Casket."
- Even though we spent winters in Mexico, do not list my next of kin as Poncho the Donkey.
- Please make sure no one knows Melissa's last words to me were, "Just sign this."
- To make my cold-as-ice WASP friends cry like the rest of the mourners, Melissa and Cooper should just tell them they've "run out of Wonder Bread."

Death doesn't scare me. I just want to leave a legacy—something sexual would be good. Take David Carradine. David became world famous for his starring role in the hit TV series *Kung Fu*, but what he's remembered for is being found dead in a Bangkok hotel, stark naked, hanging from a leather harness with a ball gag in his mouth. To this day, whenever fine acting is being discussed, Meryl Streep and Daniel Day-Lewis don't say, "David Carradine, the grasshopper guy." No. They say, "David Carradine, the asshopper guy." *That's* the kind of legacy I want to leave.

JUNE 2

Dear Diary:

Today I did something I've always wanted to do: I went shoplifting with Lindsay Lohan. Ha, ha. No, that's not a joke. In my own way I have been stealing for years. I have bath towels with big Ns on them from the Ark. However, I would never steal with Lindsay Lohan, as she is not smart. She keeps putting things down the front of her dresses even though she wears see-through dresses. Once I was told she stuffed a sofa into the back of her Spanx but was caught when she waddled out of the store with a huge butt. They thought she was Jennifer Lopez.

What I did do today was I got a tattoo! To honor the six million Jews who died in the Holocaust, on my left forearm I had them tattoo a little blue "6M." Surprisingly it hardly hurt, so next week I'm planning to get a "12M" to honor the twelve million Jews who refused to buy retail, and if *that* doesn't hurt, I'll get a "26½M" for all the Jewish businessmen whose second wives are blond shiksa goddesses.

JUNE 3

Dear Diary:

I woke up feeling yucky: headaches, coughing, chills, vomiting . . . Kind of like Amanda Bynes feels every day when she comes to. I'm fighting a cold. I called my doctor, who told me to stay in bed. So here I am at 4 p.m. watching Judge Judy berating minorities and chastising poor white trash. No matter how sick I am, a little bit of Judy makes me feel a whole lot better.

All my friends keep calling me and saying, "Oh my God, aren't you bored doing nothing?" As it turns out, the answer is no. I am loving lying here like a lox, eating Cheetos, thanking God I was wise enough to buy a caftan in no-guilt stretch fabric.

I hate people who say, "I love my work. My work is my vacation." Bullshit. Unless your "work" is lying in bed, having nude cabana boys feed you grapes and do reflexology on your feet, it is not a vacation.

And don't give me, "Oh, Joan, you're so smart, you're so well traveled—you'll be bored." Sunny von Bülow, a brilliant woman of international renown, a woman who traveled so extensively she had to renew her passport four times a year, lay in one place for twenty-eight years and not a peep, not a complaint. Never once in her 10,220 days in bed did anyone hear her murmur, "I have got to get going here; I'm bored. I have to do some volunteer work; let me go talk to some orphans at the Y."

JUNE 4

Dear Diary:

Got an early birthday card from my agent, Stunning Steve Levine. It said, "Happy Birthday, Jo . . ." He took off 10 percent; what a kidder. I also got a "Wish You Were Here" card from Forest Lawn Cemetery. I love their go-get-'em attitude.

JUNE 5

Dear Diary:

Today I was supposed to be at a surprise birthday party Melissa was throwing for me, but instead I buried my neighbor. (Later I found out she was only dozing, but I'd had enough.) In truth, my neighbor Elaine was a nice woman who had suffered from a bad case of ugly, so not so much for her, but for the people who had to look at her in the elevator and not wince, it was a blessing.

JUNE 6

Dear Diary:

Okay, I hate myself for the last entry. I said, "It was a blessing." I hate people who say that when a sick person dies. How do we know it is a blessing for them? No one wakes up from a coma and says, "Finally, I'm dying; what a blessing." What my friends say when they wake up from a coma is, "Where the fuck is my purse?" or, to the sobbing people leaning over them, "Jesus, Nana, take a breath mint. If this illness doesn't kill me, your breath will."

Elaine loved attention, which is why she flashed from her front window well into her eighties, and the saddest part is, because she was in a coma she missed all the attention. Elaine's funeral was packed. I'm not sure if it was because Elaine was truly loved or because her children used a five-star caterer and when Jews hear that there's a to-die-for buffet in town, they show up.

JUNE 7

Dear Diary:

Flew back to L.A. today to get ready for *Fashion Police* and some concerts. I'm planning to do five shows in five days. I figured out I'll be spending more time with gay men than Liza Minnelli did on her wedding nights.

JUNE 8

Dear Diary:

Today's my eightieth birthday. I made a list of the interesting things about being eighty:

1. I can bully seventy-nine-year-olds by telling them to shut the fuck up and respect their elders.
2. I can still call Betty White an old whore.
3. I've started a new business using my old tampons as party favors.
4. The dogs are blaming the smell of pee on me.
5. When young people ask me if I have started "hooking up," unfortunately they mean to life support.
6. When I reach orgasm I yell out Dr. Kevorkian's name.
7. I can put on my bra with a shoehorn.
8. I can land a big endorsement deal with industrial-strength Depends.
9. When I watch the History channel, my name comes up six or seven times a night.
10. John McCain is sexting me pictures of his junk.

JUNE 9

Dear Diary:

Poor John Travolta. There's another story in the tabloids about how gay he is. I have no idea if he's gay or not. On one hand, he has a wife and kids and does macho things like fly planes. On the other hand, he's a fabulous dresser, a great dancer and likes to be called "Miss Phillips" when he goes shopping in Talbots's Big Gals section. Maybe he and Kevin Spacey can just get married and have a very hetero honeymoon on whatever planet it is John's Scientology guru thinks we all come from.

JUNE 10

Dear Diary:

I could never be in a cult. For starters, they never accessorize properly. David Koresh had no fashion sense, Jim Jones wore leisure suits, and I don't care how charismatic Osama bin Laden was—an AK-47 and an insulin drip do not take the place of drop earrings or a well-placed brooch.

The word "charismatic" really annoys me. Journalists and pundits are quick to call every cult leader "charismatic" because they convinced thousands of demented losers to drink Kool-Aid or walk into gunfire. "Charismatic" is not a synonym for "fucking nuts." Charlie M. didn't really have "charisma"; he had LSD and boundary issues. He was also nice in his own way. Few people know this, but Chuck was a Buddhist—and a Buddhist with a sense of humor. Whenever I met him he had a real twinkle in his third eye. If he would've invited me for a long weekend at Spahn Ranch, all expenses paid, there's a fair chance I might have gone night crawling with Linda and Leslie and Susan and Tex.

JUNE 11

Dear Diary:

It's 2 a.m. and I *just* figured out why Scientology is so successful. I was having my usual dream, the one where I'm on a speedboat off of St. Barts with my new lover, Bill Gates, when the boat hits a school of sharks and flips over. Bill is immediately devoured into bits of chum by the frenzied makos, while I land safely on the back of a passing dolphin and am brought back to my private resort without so much as a hair or bangle out of place. And even more important, the tape recorder with the waterproof tape I safeguarded in my bra with Bill's last words—"I leave every dime I have to Joan Rivers"—clearly audible, is in perfect condition.

Anyway, I think Scientology caught on because L. Ron Hubbard created it. Like me, many people are drawn to individuals with initials in their names. My favorite actor is F. Murray Abraham. (It used to be Lee J. Cobb, but he's pushing daisies.) I remember the first time I met F; I said, "F, you . . . are fabulous." And he agreed.

My favorite president? Harry S. Truman. The S stood for "sexy"; Harry was one hot haberdasher. It would have been Richard M. Nixon but the M stood for "Milhous." Milhous, by the way, is Quaker for "Momma's Boy." Nixon took his mother everywhere. I'll never forget the inauguration. There was the leader of the free world dancing with her urn.

My favorite singer? k.d. lang. Not only does she make great music, but she's really handy with a hammer and nails, and can get me free tickets to *The Ellen DeGeneres Show*. Best of all, if k.d. likes you she will come over and clean your shag carpets with her tongue. And FYI, if you haven't seen her lately, she's starting to look an awful lot like Wayne Newton.

My favorite poets? T. S. Eliot and e.e. cummings. Although I must admit, e.e.'s resistance to capital letters speaks to a serious lack of healthy self-esteem. Or a broken typewriter. (This is often how genius is born. If Monet could have afforded a palette, he would not have been forced to mix his paint colors *on* the canvas; if Al Jolson didn't stutter, all of America would not have sung, "T-T-Tootsie good-bye"; and if Teddy Roosevelt's wife was not such a shopper and didn't constantly beg him for money, he would not have yelled, "Charge! All right, all right, charge.")

In fact, if Mel Gibson were P. U. Gibson, not only would I go back to seeing his movies, I might even revisit his anti-Semitic remarks.

JUNE 12

Dear Diary:

Flew to Omaha, Nebraska, for a concert tonight. I'm feeling really fat so before I disembarked the plane I pulled the seat belt into its narrowest length. This way, no matter how thin the next bitch is who sits there, when she sits down and tries to buckle up she'll have to loosen it and she'll feel fat, just like I did.

Playing the Midwest is fun but tricky. The audiences are really, really nice but really, really Waspy. They're so Christian even the women have foreskin.

JUNE 13

Dear Diary:

Show went great last night in spite of the fact that it was like playing a Bund meeting. Heading off to Topeka for the second concert on the "Watch the Jew Entertain the Gentiles" tour. Unlike Jews, gentiles keep their emotions totally within. When a Jewish mother dies, the daughter screams and beats her chest and pulls out her hair for a week. When a WASP mother dies, the daughter does a small sniffle and then says, "Pity. Who got her shoes?"

JUNE 14

Dear Diary:

In Kansas and I adore the people here. They have great pioneer hardiness. One gets to see the big sky and get a true sense of the American work ethic. Media pundits think Kansas is completely ass-backwards because the people in Kansas don't believe in things like science and math and reading and electricity and weather, but those same pundits forget that Dorothy was from Kansas. Yes, *that* Dorothy: Toto-loving, witch-killing, ruby-slipper-wearing, gay-icon Dorothy. Right-wing Kansas is the birthplace of all things gay, so how unhip could the place possibly be? If there was no Judy there would be no Liza, and if there was no Liza there would be no Betty Ford Clinic, and if there was no Betty Ford Clinic there would be no TMZ to report gossip, and if there was no gossip I'd be working as a waitress in a diner in Yonkers, New York. I *love* Kansas.

JUNE 15

Dear Diary:

I flew back to New York for a minor procedure; I'm having my lips done. Not *those* lips; the ones on my face. I need a little filler. But truly only a little. I don't want to turn into one of those Beverly Hills housewives who have so much filler in their lips that they look like ducks and the only place they fit in is Disneyland. I've never understood why those women do that. They don't look sexy. Their lips are so swollen they look like they've spent a weekend with Josh Brolin.

JUNE 16

Dear Diary:

Procedure went well. Healing quickly. I should be able to purge soft foods by 8 p.m. tonight.

JUNE 17

Dear Diary:

I think I had too much wine last night and apparently did something I should regret because I got a phone call from Meg Ryan's publicist and lawyer this morning, threatening me with a lawsuit. It seems I was so happy with my big new lips, and being under the influence of Novocain and Merlot, I called Meg and left the following message on her answering machine: "Hey, Meg, quack quack, how are your duck lips, quack quack? I think my agent can get you an audition for an Aflac commercial. Quack-fucking-quack." I'll send her an apology gift—and some pâté.

JUNE 18

Dear Diary:

About those *other* lips. I would never get a vaginal rejuvenation. At my age, the only person interested in getting inside my vagina is my probate lawyer because it's where I hide my really good jewelry.

I can't figure out how a woman knows if her vaginal walls need to be redone. My gynecologist hates to examine me because my vagina is dropping so fast that he is in danger of getting a concussion unless he wears a hard hat. I know my vagina is stretched, as a year ago I had seventy-seven Chilean miners trapped in there. Next time I go to my gynecologist, Dr. Lickapussy, I'll ask him if I need a vaginal tightening. If his answer echoes three times, I'll assume it's a yes.

JUNE 19

Dear Diary:

Good news! James Gandolfini is dead. Wait, that looks wrong. It's not good news that he's dead—he was a lovely man. But good in that a few weeks before he passed I mentioned to Melissa that I had seen him on a talk show and he didn't look well. So, should the comedy thing fall apart, I think I've got a future running a psychic hotline.

The media called James Gandolfini an American icon because he was a "murderer with a heart." Nonsense.

He was an actor playing a murderer with a heart. You know who was a murderer with a heart? John Gotti, that's who. And *his* heart used to beat at ninety beats per second because he had just ripped it out of the chest of a perfectly healthy young man who had the effrontery to look at him the wrong way in an IHOP.

Everyone was all shocked and stunned that Gandolfini died. Why? He was morbidly obese and smoked and drank like crazy. I'm surprised he lived as long as he did. Same thing with Michael Jackson. When MJ died people were acting all shocked that he kacked out. Again, why? For years he lived on a diet of propofol and small boys. How he made it to fifty is anyone's guess. How he made it to a fifth-grade homeroom at the age of forty-seven is not anyone's guess but an ongoing felony investigation.

JUNE 20

Dear Diary:

I went to my friend Beyoncé's penthouse last night and her two-year-old baby, Blue Ivy or Blue Room or Blue Balls—I'm not sure, I know it's "Blue" something—was watching *Romper Room.* I decided I hate Miss Sally. For as far back as I can remember, at the end of every show Miss Sally holds up a "magic looking glass" and says hello to various boys and girls out there in TV land. It was always, "And I see Billy and Johnny and Patty and Kim" (of course, these days it's "Joquamda and Latisha and Mohamed and Fareed"), but never once, in all these years, have I ever heard her say, "And I see Joan from Larchmont," or, "I see Joan, who is debuting on *Sullivan*," or, "I see Joan, who is having filler injections in Dr. Diamond's office."

JUNE 21

Dear Diary:

Today is the official first day of summer—which means it's also the first official day of my having to stop people on the street to say things like, "Please put on a shirt, your boobs are dragging on the sidewalk. It may not bother your wife, but you're making *me* nauseous, Mr. Feldman." Man boobs annoy me big-time. Why can't they leave us something? It's enough that men are becoming sensitive and waxing, but now they have breasts? It's not right! Poor Angelina Jolie; she never thought she would say, "I'd give my eyeteeth to look like Kevin James."

Speaking of Angelina, she's started a trend in preventative medicine. Yesterday while visiting my podiatrist, he said, "Joan, you might get a plantar wart; hey, let's take that foot off now. You can use the extra shoe as a vase." I said, "Dr. Schwartz, isn't that a bit extreme?" He stood up and said, "Not at all. Look at my body! Do I look great or what? I'm a man in my fifties and I'm wearing girls' jeans—and you know why? Because I was scared I might get a bump on my hooha so I just lopped it off!

I've never been happier. Finally, I'm a junior petite. It's a small price to pay for not standing in front of a urinal."

JUNE 22

Dear Diary:

Just got back from the drugstore. I don't usually run those kinds of errands myself, but my housekeeper took time off to sell her six-year-old daughter's kidney—at least I think that's what her note said; I don't read Esperanto. So I had to go to CVS myself. Whenever I go there I fill my cart with tampons, maxi pads and lube. Let them wonder.

JUNE 23

Dear Diary:

Went to a party last night with my agent Steve Levine's secretary's second cousin, Alan. He's an unmarried fifty-two-year-old nebbish with a lisp who made a small fortune in women's foundations. "Joan, would you like to thee thome new Thpanx?" "No sanks, Alan."

The party was a big snore. There wasn't one person there who could either advance my career or, even better, destroy the career of anyone who could even marginally be considered my peer. (By the way, I hate the word "peer," as in, "O. J. Simpson was found guilty by a jury of his peers." Unless the jury was made up of twelve rich, African-American Heisman Trophy winners who appeared in the film *The Towering Inferno*, O. J. wasn't tried by a jury of his peers; he was tried by the twelve stupidest people in the United States.)

I guess this means I really don't have any "peers," either. A handful of drag queens who do me in lounges in Vegas doesn't count. Do the math: How many *other* octogenarian female Jewish comedians with acid reflux and two cable shows do you know?

JUNE 24

Dear Diary:

Today the Supreme Court approved gay marriage! Well, they didn't actually "approve" it; it's just that five of the Supremes love going to well-catered events and don't really give a shit what the occasion is. (You haven't lived until you've witnessed Ruth Bader Ginsburg shoving baby lamb chops into her purse.) Now that I'm an ordained minister, this means more work for me, which means I won't have to go to the women's shelter when I lose all my money in a game of strip poker with Larry King.

JUNE 25

Dear Diary:

Big tribute for Don Rickles tonight at the Waldorf-Astoria. It was run by the Friars Club, which is basically a gay bar without the good-looking men. It was a tribute, not a roast, which means either (a) the Friars couldn't get a television deal to film the event, or (b) they were afraid the rich corporate pricks wouldn't buy tickets because they didn't want comedians to make fun of them in front of their underage Argentinean girlfriends.

I had a great time and got lots of laughs. Don is a lovely man and it was nice to help honor him. He laughed so hard he nearly dried his pants. A lot of big stars were there, including Bobby De Niro. And I call him "Bobby," in the same way I called John Wayne "Duke," or in the same way I call Anderson Cooper "Liza." Bobby's a good sport, especially on the jokes about his penchant for women of color, but then again, he should be. He's had more black asses on his face than the backseat of Rosa Parks's bus.

JUNE 26

Dear Diary:

I was asked to do a benefit for some group—I'm not sure which, but I'm very into charity. It turns out this charity fights teenage pregnancy. Of course I said yes. I work in Hollywood; I see how unwanted pregnancies can mess up young women's lives. They're missing out on all the fun. Teenage girls shouldn't be mothers; they should be drug addicts.

Jane Fonda is a leader in the battle against teenage pregnancy. I remember once Jane and I were having lunch (Vietnamese food of course), and she asked me what I thought was the best way for innocent teenage girls to not get pregnant. I said, "Lesbianism." Jane got very upset and said, "Teenage girls shouldn't even know about things like that yet." I said, "Then what's the best way for innocent teenage girls not to get pregnant?" She gave me that big, two-time-Oscar-winner Fonda smile, and said, "Blow jobs."

JUNE 27

Dear Diary:

I've been asked to appear in a taped segment on Israel's number-one-rated television show. They want me to do a "top ten list" about why I love Israel. At first they wanted me to go to Israel in August and I said, "Perfect. There's nothing like going to the desert in the middle of the summer." But then they figured out it would be cheaper—leave it to my people—just to film it in New York in front of some slums and we could pretend I was on the border near Palestine. So I'm working on the list.

JUNE 28

Dear Diary:

In less time than it takes to say "Shalom," Steve Levine has arranged pitch meetings for me in New York this summer with the top three TV networks in Israel: FEH, OYI and Vav Gimmel Vav.

JUNE 29

Dear Diary:

Here's my top ten list:

Top Ten Things I Love About Israel

1. I love its blue and white flag. It matches my legs.
2. I love that they have (Prime Minister) Bibi and we have (Honey) Boo Boo.
3. I love that Israel is so much closer to the South African diamond mines than New York.
4. I love Israeli men—they're tall, dark and hairy. Just like Persian women.
5. I love that Israelis, unlike New Yorkers, don't eat corned beef and pastrami with butter.
6. I love that in Israel, "Dudu" is a nickname, not an excretion.
7. I love that Israel reminds me of Boca Raton—palm trees, white sand and old Jews.
8. I love that it's not Egypt.
9. I love the Gaza Strip—it is my favorite drag name.
10. I love that the Dead Sea was named for my sex life.
11. I love that Israel has kosher McDonald's. Instead of a Big Mac they have a Big Macher.

12. I love that Israel's cows produce more milk than anyone in the world except Dolly Parton.
13. And most of all, I love that voice mail was invented in Israel. It said, "Leave a message. Or don't. I'm only your mother, I'll be dead by Tuesday, anyway."

I know, I know, there are thirteen items on the list instead of ten, but since the Israeli network execs are Jews they'll probably insist on taking something off.

JUNE 30

Dear Diary:

God, I'm on a plane, again! Melissa, Cooper and I are off to Mexico for a wedding and I almost didn't make it as I needed to update my passport. My current passport photo is a cave drawing. I'm not sure why Americans even need passports to go to Mexico. Not only do 80 percent of the people from Mexico live in America now (most of them within six blocks of Melissa's house), but I have yet to meet a customs agent who won't accept a little kindne$$ from a stranger to get into their country. I could have a bazooka on my shoulder and my tits could be ticking, but if I have a couple of pe$o$ hanging out of my purse it's *"Buenos días, Señora Rivers!"*

I hope by now you realize that this is a humor book and it's not meant to be taken seriously. If not, you can't return it because we've got your money and you're halfway through. Plus I'm sure there are stains on it you'd probably rather not explain to the credit manager.

JULY

Can you pick which one has my original nose?

JULY 1

Dear Diary:

I have just arrived at a destination wedding in Mexico. Excuse me, I mean *Meheeco.*

One of the most annoying things about Americans is that, the minute they leave the mainland, they immediately try to speak the local language, as though they were indigenous to the region, like plants and bugs and fungi. For example, in Hawaii, Mrs. Ginsburg, the Jewish fan who I met in the hotel restaurant, greeted me with, "Alloooohhhhaaaaa, Hunkaluna—want a pastrami sandwich?" In Germany, a bespectacled accountant met me with, "Willkommen to Deutschland, Fräulein Rosenberg. Oy, did I have a schmeck for lunch." And in Australia a friend of mine left me in tears, speaking the click language. I don't know what the fuck she said, except, "Click click click, Joanalah . . . Boomerang . . . Irving's dead. Click click." I didn't know if she was talking to me or chewing gum.

I know a smattering of French, but when I'm in Paris I don't try to act like the late General de Gaulle. For starters, my nose has been fixed and I don't sleep with young girls.

Anyhow, back to Mexico. First of all, who plans a wedding in Mexico in July? Even the Mexicans don't stay there; they tunnel into Arizona to cool off. Second of all,

I resent when the bride and groom call it a "destination wedding" and I have to pay to get there. It should be called a "*two* destination wedding," because long before I hit Mexico my first stop is to my bank. Between airfare, hotel and a gift, I figure this fancy-schmancy destination wedding is costing me fifteen grand to attend the nuptials of a couple whose marriage will probably last three weeks longer than my actual trip.

And, if I'm going to pay to go to a destination wedding, make it different. We've all seen Hawaii, we've all been to the Bahamas and we've all gone barefoot in the sands of Iwo Jima. I want it to be unique. *Join Fritz and Helga at their destination wedding in Auschwitz. You'll laugh, you'll learn, you'll love!* This gives a whole new meaning to the term "bridal shower." And the gift shop, believe me, is to die for.

Back to the destination wedding in Mexico. For starters the groom is half her age and rumor has it he signed the prenup in crayon. And he's already cheating on her. My friend is smart enough that the prenup will only leave him $600, a used mink coat* and a couple of tins of Friskies.

* I say "used" mink coat, not "pre-owned." "Pre-owned" is bullshit. That's like serving leftovers and calling them "pre-chewed." Used is used—like an old car, antique furniture or Marilyn Monroe's vagina.

JULY 2

Dear Diary:

Just got off the plane from my flight home from Meheeco and I'm tired and cranky. The wedding was horrible; the big attraction was hitting the piñata. There's nothing worse than watching adults whack furiously at a donkey made out of crepe paper and then push, shove and elbow each other out of the way to get some candy. "Look, it's a Jujube! Hey, after twenty swings and a crushed disc I got a Jujube." One of the bridesmaids got into a catfight with the groom's aunt over a piece of Laffy Taffy. Trust me, there wasn't a Jew in the bunch. We only push, shove and elbow each other out of the way for diamonds and a 40 percent off sale at Bergdorf. Never mind candy, if Mexicans were smart they'd fill the piñata not with Snickers but with green cards. Believe me, Pedro would've broken it open on the first whack.

The best part of the trip home was that I got to sit next to Andrea Bocelli. The guy is blind as a bat and covered with taco stains. I started to strike up a conversation with him but since he wasn't wearing dark glasses I didn't know if I was boring him or he just didn't know where to look. I asked him if he'd ever heard of Joan Rivers and he said, "I thought she was dead." I was very hurt so I did little petty things to get back at him, such as when the stewardess brought the menu around I shoved it in his hands and said, "He'll order for both of us." I just kept making guttural, engine-stalling sounds as well as pointing out the sights off the left side of the plane. Finally I leaned over to him and whispered in his ear, "Please don't say anything if you feel a little dampness; my strawberry douche is leaking. I was feeling a little yeasty yesterday."

JULY 3

Dear Diary:

Tomorrow's the Fourth of July, a day most people think of as a chance to celebrate the birth of our nation. I, however, think of it as a chance for Chinese kids to blow their fingers off with cheap fireworks.

I don't understand explosives, per se. The only explosive I deal with is colitis, and the only people who celebrate that are the manufacturers of Charmin, Depends and Glade. If you really want to see fireworks, sneak into a staff meeting run by Katie Couric. The workers on Deepwater Horizon had a less explosive work environment.

JULY 4

Dear Diary:

I woke up half an hour ago and I realized just how lucky I am to have been born in the greatest country in the world (except for Malawi, where *everything* is always on sale, including the children). As I looked out of my window and saw the streets of New York below me, I realized that the people on those streets were below me, too. And not just because I'm on the fifth floor, but because in what other country could an eighty-year-old Jewish widow buy ices from an Italian pushcart operator, get a pedicure from a Vietnamese sex slave or take a ride in a taxi driven by a Haitian ex-con hiding out from the feds? I was so overcome with emotion I called my illegal Filipino housekeeper, Pingpong, up to my room to revel with me in my happiness before I yelled at her for making my latte too strong. (The ones from the big island never learn.) I'm one lucky woman. God bless America.

JULY 5

Dear Diary:

Seeing all those American flags flying from poles and car antennas and buildings and wheelchairs yesterday, one thought crossed my mind: I hate Tommy Hilfiger. The man's made a fortune working with simple red, white and blue, but Betsy Ross, the *original* primary colors gal, got zilch, zippo, nada, the big zero. Not a fucking dime. Admittedly, she only got the flag assignment because she was banging George Washington (Martha was no looker), which makes her the Monica Lewinsky of her day. As the flag turned out to be a real winner, Betsy should have gotten something out of the deal—cash, jewelry, a time-share at Valley Forge, something. We're still draping caskets with it today. Would it have killed George to toss her a colony or a compound or a slave?

JULY 6

Dear Diary:

Worked all day on jacket patterns for QVC with a new designer who claims to be straight. He kept showing me pictures of his kids and his wife, which he kept in his pocketbook in a Hello Kitty photo album. I'm tired of "straight" designers. Don't spend all day drawing dresses and scarves and belts and then go home at night and pretend to be interested in the "little woman." Any man who knows what a peplum is, is not straight. I don't care how many wives or prop children he has; if the words "summer shift," "open toe" or "cinch belt" come out of his mouth, you can bet the dick of another "straight" designer is going in it. I want my designers gay, I want my tailors straight, I want my dry cleaners Chinese and my gynecologist blind. I don't need to be lying on an examining table and hear a doctor say, "Yucch."

JULY 7

Dear Diary:

Watched the Wimbledon tennis tournament this morning. I hate tennis. All that head turning, back and forth, back and forth. It can loosen even a good face-lift. I just stare in one direction, usually at the player who grunts less. If the ball doesn't come back, obviously the other idiot missed it. FYI: If I want to hear someone grunting, I don't need Wimbledon; I'll watch CeeLo Green try to cross his legs.

I love England, I love London, I love the royals but OMG the Brits are just not an attractive people. At least not compared to all the Botoxed celebrity types that I run with. Then again, compared to the hirsute Greeks, the peasanty Russians or the slope-browed Croats, the Brits are big-time stunning. To help me feel better about my looks I constantly remind myself that most minor races are ugly. Sometimes I pull them up on the Internet alphabetically, and every time I start to feel really homely, I just go and stand next to Miss Eskimo.

JULY 8

Dear Diary:

Today Sassy Steve Levine said I've been invited to go on *Dancing with the Stars*. I politely declined. I said, "No fucking way! What's wrong with you?" (1) I'm not a good dancer. (2) I hate touching sweaty strangers. (3) I'm deathly afraid that Bruno will jump across the judges' table and bite me in the face.

JULY 9

Dear Diary:

Today is the first day of Ramadan, which is a Muslim "holiday" where Muslims fast for thirty days. Just what we need: groups of hysterical, angry people who hate us to start with and who are now hungry on top of it. We keep sending them millions of dollars and soldiers; it's so fucking stupid. We should send them a thousand boxes of Twinkies and a little KFC; not only will they be appreciative, they'll be way too bloated and lethargic to attack us.

JULY 10

Dear Diary:

Feeling great. I just finished reading the newspaper of record in my house, the *National Enquirer*, and there was a cover story on fat celebrities. What surprised me was that the story included Keanu Reeves. I was shocked. I didn't know he was still a celebrity. I could have sworn I saw him last Tuesday making lattes at the Starbucks in Malibu. But what *really* surprised me was a picture of Renée Zellweger. Not only was her face pulled so tight that she could whisper in her own ear, but because of her weight gain her eyes, which had always been a little squinty, now looked so Chinese that the U.S. government is questioning her country of origin on her passport. If the fat pushes her squinty eyes up any more I predict she'll go from being an A-list movie star to being the next Mrs. Woody Allen. I say this with love: I really like that little prune face. I remember when Renée starred in *Bridget Jones's Diary* and she made a big stink about how she gained twenty pounds for the part because she was devoted to her "craft." Big fucking deal. Shelley Winters gained eighty pounds making *The Poseidon Adventure* because she was devoted to craft services.

JULY 11

Dear Diary:

We're starting to plan Grandma Week with Cooper. Every year he and I go somewhere special, just the two of us . . . plus my publicist, assistant, stylist, and hair and makeup people, and of course Pingpong. It sounds like a lot but we hardly notice them, as Cooper and I sit in first class, and they all take turns sharing a seat in coach. The time away with Cooper is great as it also gives Melissa and me a breather before we appear on Discovery ID as the lead story in a "Daughters Who Kill" segment. I don't think she has it in for me—although for my birthday she bought me a bathing suit made out of lead—but I know things. Last year I had walking . . . well, limo-ing pneumonia and the doctor came out to the waiting room and said to Melissa, "I just need to know, God forbid, are you prepared for your mother's death?" And Melissa said, "Prepared? I've had a shovel in my trunk since 1983. The Boy Scouts aren't this prepared."

There are ways to tell your family is sick of you:

- They take the batteries out of your Clapper when you're dying to sleep.

- They find you a hospice nurse on Craigslist.
- They turn your room into a storage space while you're still living in it.
- At Thanksgiving they put you in the oven to check on the turkey.
- They send you on vacation to Guantánamo Bay.

JULY 12

Dear Diary:

It's 800 fucking degrees in New York and the city smells worse than Precious after a six-day cleanse. It's so hot even the fragrance-schprizters in Saks are starting to smell like the homeless.

And yet so many politicians and preachers are saying they don't believe in climate change and think that the world is collapsing because God hates homos. If God wanted to "punish homosexuals," as Pat Robertson said, then why did he make the tsunami in Japan, or the earthquake in Haiti? Doesn't God have a GPS? If God hated homos, those catastrophes were such a waste of his efforts. Why didn't he just flood Key West with cotton-poly blends or, even worse, open a Walmart in West Hollywood? That would've stopped those gay guys dead. I find it hard to believe that God's melting the planet because a couple of florists in Palm Springs added baby's breath to an arrangement.

JULY 13

Dear Diary:

I was watching *The View* or *The Talk* or *The Chew* . . . I can't remember which one, they're all the same except that *The Chew* has burping. So I was watching and one of the hosts said about one of those young, interchangeable actresses no one can really identify, "I don't begrudge her success." And I thought, *Neither do I.* This girl obviously worked very hard for it—just look at how raw her knees are.

The only person whose success I begrudge is Mother Teresa, that underdressed, poorly coiffed, androgynous old bag. People carried on about what a wonderful, giving person Mother Teresa was because she washed the feet of the poor. I say, wash the feet of one poor person and you're kind; two, you're doing a mitzvah; three or more, face it, Big T, you've got a fetish. She did it because she liked it. Terry washed the feet of millions, yet not one reporter ever mentioned that when she was finished scrubbing the heels of the downtrodden, she always lit up a cigarette and sang a Johnny Mathis tune.

JULY 14

Dear Diary:

It's Bastille Day in France, marking the day when millions of French people stormed the Bastille protesting Jerry Lewis's upcoming tour. They celebrate with a huge military parade. Of course, being French, they march backwards down the Champs-Élysées, in full retreat.

JULY 15

Dear Diary:

Just watched back-to-back episodes of *True Blood* and *The Walking Dead*, and I'm fed up with vampires. They're everywhere: movies, TV, museums. Enough already! If I want the life sucked out of me I'll spend a long weekend with Bethenny Frankel.

How many vampires do we need? I was hunky-dory after Dracula; my desire for cave dwellers was sated. But now, suddenly there's this popular resurgence in bloodthirsty old bats that just won't die. Which reminds me, I have to set my TiVo for the season premiere of *Hot in Cleveland*. I used to always watch *True Blood* on HBO, but after six seasons, Ryan Kwanten has still not showed off his junk, yet Anna Paquin won't stop showing hers. And I really don't understand the *Twilight* series. I've seen all the movies and they bore the shit out of me. The only good part is watching Kristen Stewart suck the blood out of the director through his penis.

JULY 16

Dear Diary:

Summer is upon us, and you know what that means: people in restaurants in tank tops and halters. Uck! I don't want to look at your unkempt armpit when I've got a mouthful of angel-hair pesto. And the first part of "halter" is "halt," as in "Halt! Go back in your closet and put on a fucking blouse. Or if you're fat: a bedspread or a boat cover."

JULY 17

Dear Diary:

Just read an article that said who we are is determined in the first five years of life because our brain has grown to 86 percent of its capacity by that age. I don't believe this. I don't think that 86 percent of our entire personality is formed by age five. C'mon, are you trying to tell me that at four and a half Jeffrey Dahmer decided that instead of eating Gerber baby food he'd much rather eat the Gerber baby? Plus, if this is true, explain that kid in the movie *Mask* to me. That kid's head kept growing and growing and growing. By the time he was eleven he was blowing his nose on the drapes. His poor mother, who looked a lot like Cher, spent more on hats than rent, car and utilities combined.

JULY 18

Dear Diary:

My agent wants to book me on a lesbian cruise. I told him I'd let him know. The money's good but I'm not sure I want to spend two hours staring at a group of angry women who think nothing's funny except jokes about Antonin Scalia, Martina Navratilova or three-quarter-inch drill bits.

JULY 19

Dear Diary:

I turned on the TV hoping to find *Yentl* (I love watching Barbra Streisand magically transform from a homely girl to a homely boy), and instead I got a commercial for ChristianMingle, the dating website for happy, perky young Christians. The announcer says, "Find out God's match for you." What if God had been drinking, or Jesus double-dared him, or God was auditioning for *Punk'd* so he deliberately made a bad match for you with a pasty hunchback with a clubfoot and money problems? Should you marry him just because God says "Go" and be nauseous and miserable every time this guy wants to climb on top of you in the biblical way? Or should you date the quarterback with the great smile and big dick and then eventually marry a Jewish millionaire with mommy issues and high cholesterol? Seems like a no-brainer.

Since good Christians aren't supposed to think about, have, or enjoy sex, I can't imagine what the attraction to that website would be.

> Hi, I'm Chad McWhitey, and I'm a young Christian trying to find God's match for me. I go to a Christian

college where I'm taking Christian classes like "Don't Do That, You'll Go Blind," "Intolerance Is a Good Thing" and "Your Penis Is Just for Peeing." I have a part-time job as a cook in a non-Jew deli where my specialty sandwich is pastrami on white bread with butter—and I love to serve it with a teeming glass of whole milk! Mmmmmm!!! My hobbies include thinking about Jesus, drawing pictures of Jesus, talking to Jesus and wondering why Jesus never met God's perfect match for himself. If you want to have a clean, wholesome, sex-free experience, HMU! We can pray together!* Praise the Lord.

ChristianMingle is much different than JDate, the website where Jews go to meet and complain.

Hi. My name is Elliott. I'm good-looking in a Semitic way (thanks to my mother's side) and have a share in the family dry goods business (thanks to my father's side). My hobbies include going to nice restaurants, taking nice vacations, having a nice house within twenty miles of a big city (but not the bad ones) and schtupping my nephew's camp counselor, Rivka, twice a month. I'm looking for a buxom, appreciative Sabra with dead parents.

* Maybe it's just me, but in my eighty years on earth, I've never once dated a man who wanted me on my knees so I could pray.

JULY 20

Dear Diary:

Today was Natalie Wood's birthday. If she had either learned to swim or vacationed in a desert, today she'd be close to 804 years old. And if Elvis were alive today, he'd be close to 492 pounds.

JULY 21

Dear Diary:

Off to do a show in Nashville, which is like Branson, Missouri, with teeth. I'm looking forward to it. Country audiences are so much fun; they embrace you just like you were one of their underage cousins.

Nashville is a city that really loves its celebrities and it seems every country star has a museum there. I love museums; they can be full of fun when they accurately reflect their location and give their patrons art they can relate to. For example, in New York the Metropolitan Museum has a da Vinci that depicts Ben-Hur riding around in a chariot, looking for a parking space. The world-renowned Pepe Museum in Mexico City has the same theme painted by Frida Kahlo in which Ben is driving a Chevy with stolen plates. And perhaps the most famous museum of all, the Getty in Los Angeles, has Michelangelo's *Last Supper*, done originally as a triptych. The third panel features a vegan salad bar in the background, which art historians say explains Jesus's lanky physique.

In Branson, they had a museum called Barbara Mandrell Country, which was a shrine to the most talented yet least attractive of the Mandrell sisters. There was an exhibit of exact miniature replicas of all of her houses, complete with little barns and little animals. And in the little bathroom there's even a little toilet with teeny tiny turds.

The most incredible item in the museum was the nightgown Barbara wore on her wedding night with her husband, "Kinny" ("Kenny" to the rest of us), which is prominently displayed in a glass case right next to the fender they pulled out of her head from that car crash in '84. That nightie was shredded and tattered like she'd been attacked by a pack of wolves. I wonder if she and Kinny met on ChristianMingle.

Another museum I visited was the Ferlin Husky Wings of a Dove Museum and Prayer Theater. In addition to having all of Ferlin's memorabilia on display, every day they do musical shows based on Bible stories. I loved every minute of it even though I was very surprised to find out that the Lord had serious pitch problems.

I'm a huge country western fan, in fact I'm a bit of a C&W connoisseur and I know almost all of the original lyrics and titles. Tammy Wynette, happy about a tax break she received, originally wrote "Stand By Your Jew Accountant." Johnny Paycheck's wife, furious that his mistress got a genuine mink stole for Christmas, screamed, "Take This Cloth Coat and Shove It." But perhaps my favorite is one that Willie Nelson sings only in private or at special parties, "I'm Cryin' in My Sleep 'Cause I Found You with My Sheep."

JULY 22

Dear Diary:

The shows in Nashville were great. I love that all the shows in town were performed at 3 p.m., this way a couple can get up in the morning, hose down the double-wide, gun down a couple of defenseless animals, burn an abortion clinic, see a terrific show and still get out in time for lupper.

Now off to New Orleans, another fave of mine. Love, love, love the Big Easy. (I'm talking about the city, not what they call Taylor Swift behind her back.) The people of New Orleans love me as much as I love them. Even during Katrina they came out and supported me. I don't want to brag, but they gave me a floating ovation.

JULY 23

Dear Diary:

Concert went fine but the VIP meet and greet was a horror show. By the way, the term "VIP" means different things to different people. To casino owners, VIPs are high rollers—usually Arabian businessmen who gamble away the millions they've made screwing small American businesses. To me VIPs are those casino owners who can book me for private parties for those businessmen. One of the VIPs had really bad gas, and every time he began to speak he'd let one go. I don't know how much falafel he'd eaten, but he nearly blew the flowers off their stems. And because he was a high roller I couldn't say anything, not even something subtle like, "Excuse me, Camel-ass, while we're together is there any chance you could stuff a burka up your bunghole?" So I just smiled, dabbed my eyes with my scarf and flapped my arms like one of Jerry's kids who's been at the telethon too long and is starting to act out.

JULY 25

Dear Diary:

Just got home and I can't wait to take a bath and hop into bed. There's nothing better than curling up in your own bed with a dog you love. Now I know what Justin Theroux must see in Jennifer Aniston.

JULY 26

Dear Diary:

I love my dogs. They make me smile and laugh the way pretty-colored candy makes slow children grin and drool. I think the world would be a happier place if everybody had dogs rather than slow children—except for Koreans. If they have a dog it's usually on a bun, with a house salad and a side of fries. Yesterday at the nail salon my manicurist offered me half of a Bacon, Lassie and Tomato sandwich.

Now let's talk lesbians. They should not have dogs,

and if they do, the only dog a lesbian should have is a Pit Bulldyke. Lesbians are much more comfortable around cats. And it's not just the meowing they like; they take comfort in the fact that even if their pretty young girlfriend has left them for a middle-aged, mannish crossing guard named Stella, someone in the house is still licking pussy.

JULY 27

Dear Diary:

For purely business purposes, I went to a party tonight with my agent, S. S. (Shifty Steve) Levine. Actually, I went with Steve's cousin Ruth's morbidly obese stepson, Geoffrey. I can't stand people who spell Jeffrey "Geoffrey." It's so pretentious, just like people who spell Steven "Stephen." The biggest offender in the pretentious name game is Pink, whose real name is Vagina.

Geoffrey's having a midlife crisis and wants to give up his semi-lucrative podiatry practice to become a cowboy. Geoffrey, who tips the scales at three hundred pounds and can no longer bend down to touch his patients' toes, said he's always admired the Lone Ranger.

This is insane. I don't know how Geoffrey—or anybody—ever looked up to the Lone Ranger. He was a liar. Just calling himself "lone"? The man had a fantastic love life. Are we all forgetting about his unusual friendship with Tonto? Hello?? Yes, he could have been alone;

he had that odor from his discharge coming from his bleeding anal fissures (Silver was a very rough ride, and after three days in the saddle even the best of us gives off a slightly sour grapefruit odor). And true, any man who wears a small black mask *all the time*, even to book signings and PTA functions, is not someone to idolize or hang out with on a regular basis—he's someone to put on Megan's List—but he had no right to go whining about how "lone" he was.

I'll give you lone. My elevator man Manolo has the right to call himself lone. Every time I get into that car I hear the same thing. "No one really cares about me, señora. They get into my elevator on the third or fourth floor and say, 'How ya' doin' today, Manolo?' and just as I start to really explain why I have that rash on my hand, we hit the lobby and they're out like a bullet and I'm left talking to an empty car." *That's* lone.

JULY 28

Dear Diary:

Geoffrey has called twice to see if I'd like to go out with him again. How do I politely tell him, "It's not you, but the cheesy smell coming from under your folds reminds me of milk and I'm lactose intolerant"? It's not that he's fat; a lot of thin people smell, too. Mother Teresa never used deodorant. The only ones who could stand to be around her were lepers, because they had no noses. I wonder if that's why Taylor Swift can't keep a boyfriend. Maybe she's a "naturalist" and believes nature secretes its own washboards. Or maybe she's so busy touring she doesn't have time to douche. According to the tabloids (which I need more than water, air, or Botox), Taylor's been dumped more often than a vegan on a cabbage cleanse. Maybe she should stop composing, drop her pen, pull down her thong and take a sniff. If she doesn't, she's going to end up lone.

JULY 29

Dear Diary:

On the plane back to L.A. to see Melissa and Cooper and am watching *Into Thin Air*, the movie about climbing Mount Everest. I never understood why people do that—not climb mountains, that's the easy part; it's the schlepping all the way to Nepal I don't get. It's eighteen hours. The only mountains I was willing to schlep to were the Catskills, and that was only in their heyday, and only at the Concord Hotel, and only for a weekend (Friday one show, Saturday two), and only for really good money. And I didn't need a yak and a Sherpa and oxygen tanks to get there. Just a limo, a driver, and a tight forty minutes.

The idiots who climb Mount Everest say they do it because "it's there." Which is exactly what Pam Anderson said about Tommy Lee. And all of these rich country-club pricks who reach the summit carry on like they're the first person to do it and that they did it alone. Excuse me, don't the Sherpas do this three times a month, on foot, carrying *your* equipment because you wouldn't be able to pat yourself on the back if your hands were full? Why don't the Sherpas get any credit? Behind every good man may be a woman, but behind every good climber is a Sherpa, just as behind every good chorus boy is another chorus boy with a couple of poppers and an eight ball.

JULY 30

Dear Diary:

Melissa and Cooper took me to dinner tonight at a new, hip Chinese restaurant, Madame Mao's Moo Shu Mansion. The place is uber-Chinese. When I asked for a fork instead of chopsticks they were horrified. You'd have thought I'd asked them for their two smallest children to ship back to New York to work in my jewelry factory.

Melissa said, "Use the chopsticks, the duck tastes better." I said, "Better than what? When it was alive and quacking?" She said, "Using chopsticks enhances the experience." By that logic if I go to an Icelandic restaurant should I beat the fish against a rock before I dig in? Or if I go to an Ethiopian restaurant should I scavenge the floor for crumbs and then go to the American restaurant next door and beg for food?

JULY 31

Dear Diary:

I was watching the local news this morning and the cap-toothed, overly bronzed anchorman said, "Today is July thirty-first, Wednesday, which is Hump Day." I had no idea what he was talking about. Hump Day? I didn't know if I was supposed to ride a camel, hunt down and mount a strange man or send a birthday card to a hunchback. Who talks like this? I can't imagine Brian Williams suggesting that I "get me some loving" during his live broadcast from a bombed-out airfield in Kabul. I'm sick of friendly news anchors with their inside jokes and coy asides. They try to humanize the news. Don't. Just tell it to me. I don't need Savannah on the *Today* show saying, "The forest fire destroyed three hundred homes, and yet little seven-year-old Billy Simpson managed to find time to play with his toys in the smoldering rubble." That's *not* the story. Just give me the facts, don't try to give me the emotional pull or happy ending. In my day, after JFK was shot in Dallas, Walter Cronkite did not turn to the camera and say, "On a happier note, Jackie found a twenty-four-hour dry cleaner who got the stains out and she amortized that expensive pink suit and was able to wear it on the plane home."

Speaking of what annoys me on TV, at the end of concerts or sporting events, I'm tired of the directors cutting to shots of cheering fans. I don't need to see the fans. I want to see the big moment, when in victory, Roger Federer gives Rafael Nadal the finger, or when

Elton John thinks the curtain's down and opens the piano and pulls out a gigantic sandwich. I don't need to see fat-ass Lenny from the Bronx cheering when Alex Rodriguez hits a home run. I want to see A-Rod try to hide the syringe in his pocket while he rounds the bases.

AUGUST

This ain't the first time I've been on top of Teddy Roosevelt's face.

AUGUST 1

Dear Diary:

Tomorrow starts Grandma Week and I can't wait. Every year I hit the road with Cooper for ten days, and August is the perfect time because all of the psychiatrists, psychologists and social workers in New York City take the entire month off, leaving their wacked-out, crazy patients to roam the streets freely in hot, humid weather without counseling, supervision or Xanax.

AUGUST 2

Dear Diary:

Cooper and I are headed off to see some of the oldest and most famous historic sights in America: Mount Rushmore, the Grand Canyon, Arches National Park and my kindergarten class.

AUGUST 4

Dear Diary:

We're at the Grand Canyon. One of the other tourists said he's "never seen a hole that big." I'm guessing he's never seen Michelle Duggar's uterus.

I may not be writing much this week—Cooper and I are just going to enjoy driving through the heartland of America watching people with no chic toiling away on their farms and growing stuff.

AUGUST 6

Dear Diary:

Today we went to Mount Rushmore and the place was mobbed with tourists. I had a scuffle right away. The tour guide told us it was open seating and suddenly hundreds of Asians with cameras rushed to the front. It was very upsetting to me. I tried to explain to a forest ranger that this is an American monument and I think Americans should sit up front—unless they're very tall and they want to sit in front of me, in which case, fuck 'em. I finally played the Famous Face card and moved to a front-row seat. Loudly. I pointed out to everybody what the monument is all about (and by "everybody" I mean a guy named Ming Na and his family who I felt were Asians, because of their bound feet and funny clothes with strange fasteners instead of buttons):

1. George Washington was our first president who crossed the Delaware River and was able to do it uninterrupted because it wasn't a Carnival cruise.

2. Teddy Roosevelt, who charged up San Juan Hill in record time because there was a Jehovah's Witness running behind him badgering him to buy copies of *The Watchtower* magazine.
3. And Abe Lincoln and Thomas Jefferson, who were probably our two greatest presidents . . . one who freed the slaves and one who fucked them.

AUGUST 8

Dear Diary:

We're in Utah today. I wanted Cooper to see and press the flesh of all the people who buy Marie Osmond's doll collections. We drove directly to Arches National Park, which turned out to be a huge disappointment. Not one rock collection in the shape of a foot. What are they talking about?

Our tour guide was wearing shorts, boots and turquoise jewelry in the blazing sun, and looked stupid. I hate straight men who wear turquoise jewelry. If I see that I know he's either an alcoholic Navajo or he's toe-tapping in the men's room just off the beaten path.

AUGUST 10

Dear Diary:

Today was our last day of Grandma Week and Cooper wanted to go white-water rafting down the Colorado River. I'd have been much happier sitting in the Four Seasons watching *Deliverance* on Netflix, but whatever, it's his vacation.

Turns out the rafting trip was great—we got soaked and bumped and bruised but Cooper had a blast; and even though I'm a little battered from the rough waters and the rocks, I know I have a nice insurance claim and negligence lawsuit to file when I get home. Another win-win!

FYI: If I have to hear one more story about how brave the Western pioneers were . . . how they had to get their rafts across the crocodile-filled swirling rapids; how they had to figure out which snakes were poisonous and which ones would make lovely handbags; blah, blah, blah. You want a pioneer? Helena Rubinstein: She invented hypoallergenic, waterproof foundation and cover-sticks, so all of those Brokeback Mountain cowboys could "pioneer" each other in the back of a tent without having to worry about blackheads or combination skin.

AUGUST 12

Dear Diary:

I'm a reader. Often I'll read an entire book cover to cover in one sitting in the bathroom, which really annoys the other passengers on a plane, but as Count Vronsky said when Anna Karenina begged him not to leave her, "Too fucking bad." Apparently word of my voracious reading habits got out, and so yesterday I did an interview about my last book, *I Hate Everyone . . . Starting with Me*. I was asked who my favorite and least favorite authors are. For my favorite I said Ann Rule, the great true crime writer, even though Edith Wharton was a close second. Both are so similar. In Wharton I can watch rich society people suffer, but Rule wins because I can watch trailer trash not only suffer but get brutally murdered, sometimes hacked up or left totally unrecognizable when they're fished out of a marsh.

Both are great, cozy, good bedtime reading after a difficult day.

Again, when it came to naming my least favorite author, I had to say, "I have two!" Charles Dickens and little Anne Frank. Let's start with Dickens. What a bore. Charlie could spend eight pages describing a street in London. His novel *David Copperfield* is 1,016 pages—and no pictures! And as for Anne Frank, go back to the January 4 entry.

AUGUST 13

Dear Diary:

This is why I hate L.A. I saw a $400,000 chauffeur-driven Bentley in front of a Supercuts. I didn't even know Phil Spector was out on bail.

I am very careful about where I go to get my hair cut in Beverly Hills. I only go to regular hair salons because if you go where stars go you might catch something. I'm not saying she's dirty, but I heard that when they cut Helena Bonham Carter's hair, it made three rats homeless.

AUGUST 14

Dear Diary:

Flew back to New York last night. Didn't need an Ambien, a glass of wine or a seat next to an actuary to fall asleep. The movie on board was *All Is Lost* with Robert Redford. Other than seagulls cooing and waves splashing—and my snoring—it was basically a silent movie. Eight minutes in I was hoping the boat would capsize and Big Red would get eaten by a school of sharks that don't mind moles or bad plastic surgery.* The only thing worse would have been if Bobby were trying to pass time on the boat by reading a Dickens novel out loud.

AUGUST 16

Dear Diary:

Today is Madonna's birthday. Now I know why they refer to August as "the dog days of summer." I wasn't sure what to buy her, but I finally settled on *Fifty Shades of Grey* for her so she can read it, and a box of crayons so her boyfriend can color it in.

AUGUST 17

Dear Diary:

I can't stand people who don't pick up after their dogs. It's filthy, it's disgusting and it's unsanitary. It makes the sidewalks unsleepable for the homeless, and even worse, it forces me to wear high heels on occasions that desperately call for flats.

I *always* pick up after my dogs. Well, actually I, Joan Rivers, diva-philanthropist of a sort, amazingly sexual

---

* "Big Red" is actually a misnomer for Robert Redford. Robert Redford is not big. He's short. He's my height if I'm in heels, but I can't call him "Little Red," because that name's already been taken by Mickey Rooney's penis.

for her age, don't pick up my dogs' poo. I have my staff do it. In this case it's Pingpong's second cousin, Kabuki, who's here on a temporary visa or maybe it's an amnesty application having something to do with ivory hunting or sex trafficking. I don't know; after seeing *Downton Abbey* I make it my business not to get into backstairs gossip.

Kabuki is a lovely young Pygmy man. He has to jump up in order to hand me my mail, but I find him totally trustworthy. Not once in all the time he's been scooping the poop has he ever brought one of my dogs to a Korean restaurant and "accidentally" left him in the kitchen.

AUGUST 18

Dear Diary:

Back in L.A. Everyone is just starting to calm down. There was an earthquake here last night. Very scary! Everything started to shake. Only two people were happy about the quake: Michael J. Fox, as it was the first time in years he walked straight; and me. Now that my vagina has dropped so low, I just suctioned it to the floor of my bedroom and was perfectly safe. Never thought I would say this, but hooray for age.

AUGUST 19

Dear Diary:

Performed at a women's show and it went surprisingly well. Lena Dunham spoke about how difficult it is to be a woman in our business and claims she, and she alone, has broken through for women. In the audience Tina Fey, Amy Poehler, Barbara Walters, Diane Sawyer, Mary Tyler Moore and Sarah Jessica Parker all started to cry because according to that fatso, they didn't count. I do want to give her credit however—Lena was the first fat girl naked on television and she changed the way America looks at their TV sets. They now do it with their hands over their eyes.

AUGUST 20

Dear Diary:

I have to send a gift to the Royal Family. I totally missed Prince William and Princess Kate's son George's birthday. Little Georgie has William's full lips and Kate's sparkling eyes. I hope he doesn't have Diana's sense of direction. It's very hard to buy a gift for the future king of England. What do you get someone who already owns Scotland? I went into a store to buy him a set of blocks and they said, "He's already got Trafalgar Square and Regent Street."

Our royal family—the Obamas, not the Kardashians—welcomed a new addition into their family, too.

No, Sasha's not pregnant—but wouldn't it be fabulous if she were? She could be the first baby mama on Obama-care. President Obama has gotten a new dog. I could tell right away he was Obama's dog: He was cute and black, and when he barked, no foreigners listened.

AUGUST 21

Dear Diary:

Just got to San Francisco for a concert. Should be fun, it'll be my crowd: fifteen thousand gay guys and the fat gal pals they dance with.

San Francisco is *still* the gayest city in the country, hands down—or bottoms up, depending on who took the poppers! This city is so gay that at the bar in my hotel the specialty drink is the AIDS cocktail.

AUGUST 22

Dear Diary:

Oy. On the way to my show tonight we got stuck on a bridge behind a car with handicap plates.

What is the driver's handicap? Does he have only one leg and therefore can't brake? Or tiny little dwarf hands and can't turn the wheel? Maybe he's got Tourette's and every time he—shitfuck, shitfuck, shitfuck—twitches, the car keeps switching lanes? Does he have to stop and scratch while going seventy miles per hour because he has the heartbreak of psoriasis? Is he deaf? Because I remember when driving with Helen Keller the guy driving behind us kept honking his horn. He figured out it was a complete waste of time when he hit the ditch.

I think handicap plates should be more specific. Right now all they have is a drawing of a wheelchair. I think if the driver is blind, the plate should have a picture of Stevie Wonder; and if he's retarded, a picture of Sarah Palin; and if it's an underage driver, a picture of R. Kelly with a line through it.

I was getting agitated when I noticed the driver also had a bumper sticker that read, "I'd rather be fishing." So I hit him in the rear and knocked him off the bridge into the water. I got to my gig in Sausalito and he got a guppy on his way to God. Win-win!

AUGUST 23

Dear Diary:

My concert went really well; God bless the San Fran homos! If she's still alive, I'll bet Anita Bryant is sorry she dissed them. At the end of the show, all fifteen thousand party bottoms stood up and gave me a farting ovation.

AUGUST 25

Dear Diary:

I may be changing agents even though I love Suave Steve Levine. I think of agents the way I think of a pair of old Spanx: (1) They're not as bright as when you first got them; (2) they sure don't support you the way they did in the beginning; and (3) after a couple of months they really start to smell. I think the real reason I'm leaving is because I hate my agent's new assistant, Helmut. He's a little snot that prides himself on his candor and frankness. Honestly, I don't want candor and frankness from a twelve-year-old with rich parents and hair gel. I don't need, right before I go on, him whispering in my ear, "Fingers crossed you still remember your act, Miss Rivers," or, "Know why I like you? You make my nana look hot!" I want someone who will be kissing my ass so much they'll have to travel with a suitcase filled with Blistex. Never mind a good-looking kid from a rich family; I want a delusional adult with low self-esteem and people-pleasing issues. I want to hear, "Oh, Miss Rivers, you are so much more beautiful and thin in person!" rather than, "Gee, even in clothes your body looks like it's melting."

AUGUST 26

Dear Diary:

Chilling at Melissa's house after spending all day tending to business. While watching Congress on C-SPAN tonight, I had a revelation. (I don't normally watch C-SPAN but my remote froze while I was changing channels trying to find *Animal Horror Stories* and *Pets Who Kill.*) The revelation is this: When a member of Congress refers to another member as "my distinguished colleague," what he means is "that dim-witted asshole," and when he says "with all due respect," he means "fuck you and the lobbyist you rode in on." I love America.

AUGUST 27

Dear Diary:

I took Cooper to SeaWorld in San Diego today. We went swimming with the dolphins. I love dolphins. They're smart and they're beautiful, but what nobody talks about is that they shit in the water. As Elie Wiesel likes to say, "Never again."

AUGUST 28

Dear Diary:

The Elie Wiesel quote got me thinking. As Hitler's niece, Bertha von Schnitzel, once told me, "It's very hard to cheer up Holocaust victims. Joan, no matter how many times I'm in their company and no matter how hard I try, I just can't put a positive spin on their experiences. What can you say?" And she's right, what *can* you say to Buchenwald Betty and Auschwitz Arnie?

- “Hey, could be worse. At least you got three hots and a cot!”
- “Look how easy it was to keep your weight down! I’ll bet not one person in the camps ever came up to you and said, ‘Ruthie, you look a little hippy. Lay off the dirt soup.’”
- “Don’t be a whiner—you can finally pull off horizontal stripes!”
- “So they put you on a train in the middle of the night and moved you out of your house. What’s so bad? No one likes to summer where they winter!”

AUGUST 29

Dear Diary:

Went to a big Hollywood party tonight and guess who snubbed me? Gayle King. That’s right, Gayle King. With all due respect, I spent all night chatting with Jane Fonda, Lily Tomlin, Robert De Niro and Martin Scorsese, but *Gayle King* ignored me??? Maybe she’s mad at me because I’m always making jokes about her friendship with Oprah, or maybe it’s because when I saw her at the party I said, “Gayle, I love your chunky silver bracelet. Are you wearing a matching cock ring?” Whatever. I still consider her a distinguished colleague.

AUGUST 30

Dear Diary:

I took Cooper to the Dodgers' game tonight. He had a great time. The Dodgers' pitcher was a Korean rookie named Hyun-Jin Ryu, so the stands were packed with Korean fans. I felt like an extra on *The Bridge on the River Kwai.** The Dodgers won and Ryu was terrific. The only bad thing was when we went to the food court, the famous Dodger Dogs still had their tails.

AUGUST 31

Dear Diary:

I'm on the plane flying home. It's the last day of August, which means it's safe to be in New York because all the shrinks are back from the Hamptons and the crazies are back in therapy. But just my luck, I'm seated next to Gary Busey and Charlie Sheen. I'm praying the movie is *All Is Lost.*

---

* I know, I know: The River Kwai is in Thailand, but I'm not good at geography. Up until last year I thought *Apocalypse Now* took place in Flemington, New Jersey.

SEPTEMBER

Four fab supermodels. Or as I think of them, one hundred pounds of fun!

SEPTEMBER 1

Dear Diary:

Today starts Pilot Season, which is the busiest time of year for actors, flight attendants and anyone else who wants to do a pilot. I'll be heading to L.A. in a few days because that's where most of the pilots are shot (except for the ones leaving airports in Afghanistan). I don't usually go up for roles these days (I used to go down for them but you can see where that got me—doing one-nighters in Milwaukee for old Shriners and their nurses). I'm in a very bad place in my career for pilot casting. On one end, that old has-been Judi Dench gets offered all the feisty-tough-talking-adorable-wise-been-through-it-all granny roles, and on the other end of the spectrum, that young whore Diane Keaton gets offered all the if-you-squint-and-keep-the-lights-low-I-still-look-good-enough-to-have-one-fuck-left-in-me mother roles.

My old agent, Steve Levine, always said that I should be more interested in getting shows produced than in being in them. "Joan," he'd say, "producing will bring you passive income." I'd say, "Steve, you sound like a lazy prostitute." He'd answer, "Joan, look at the bright side—you don't have to 'do lunch' with the johns. You just have to 'do' them." So just as soon as my stitches heal (I had a small procedure yesterday; I had my left ass cheek removed from my ankle), I'm going to put on my thinking cap and come up with some show ideas to pitch to the networks.

SEPTEMBER 2

Dear Diary:

Today's Labor Day, the day we honor Kate Gosselin, the Octomom and any other woman who's spent more time in hard labor than a mouthy prisoner at Leavenworth.

Labor Day has always been very close to my heart because I get to honor those wonderful adult workers in Thailand who make a dollar a week cutting, buffing and polishing the jewelry I sell on QVC, jewelry that they themselves could *never* hope to afford. But what I like most about Labor Day is that it's the day of the year when sloppy men and fat women are no longer allowed to wear white, which allows the rest of us nicely appointed, well-groomed citizens never to have to vomit in our mouths again.

I believe the "No white after Labor Day" rule was created by rich people who like to get away from the city and go to their summer compounds where they'd wear light-colored clothing so they wouldn't sweat under the hot sun on their yachts. Or Paula Deen created it in a wild overreaction to the scandal involving the N-word.

I did a little research and discovered that the Labor Day holiday was created in 1894 by Peter J. McGuire, who was a member of the Brotherhood of Carpenters. (He's not to be confused with Karen Carpenter of the Carpenters, who founded the Let's Starve Ourselves to Death holiday in 1983.) Everyone thinks Peter was a staunch union organizer who believed in the greater good and created this holiday to honor the brave efforts of the workers who were standing up for their rights against "The Man." The truth is he just wanted a day off to drink and bang the little chippie he kept in a walk-up near Union Square without his wife knowing.

I'm heading off to a party in the Hamptons, which I love. I always feel better about myself coming home when I have really nice silverware in my purse.

SEPTEMBER 3

Dear Diary:

Just got on the plane to head to L.A. Had a great time in the Hamptons, BBQ-ing with people I loathe. The Hamptons are like Heidi Klum's vagina—a place where lots of diverse rich people go for fun, but Jews are not really welcome.

The Hamptons are also filled with second wives who are very easy to spot; just check out their rings. First wives' rings are always little bitty chips; the second wives have rings the size of NeNe Leakes's ass.

The guy sitting next to me on the plane started getting all chatty, but I cut that off right away. He started waxing on about lawn care so I pulled out my private collection of Yoko Ono CDs and said, "Wanna listen?" He put on a sleep mask and headphones and stuffed a sock in his mouth. And I couldn't blame him; even John Lennon, when he heard Yoko's first CD, said, "Yoko, oh no!" Should be a pleasant flight.

SEPTEMBER 4

Dear Diary:

Had twenty-five minutes between *Fashion Police* and *Joan & Melissa: Joan Knows Best?* tapings, so I headed over to the plastic surgeon's office for a quickie. I've had so many procedures done I've spent more time in surgery than the doctors on *Grey's Anatomy*. I've been pulled so tight that the last time my doctor asked for a urine sample I just cried into a bottle. I've been pulled tighter than Mary-Kate Olsen's belt. Yes, I admit it; I've been given more lifts than Aileen Wuornos. It's reached the point where I've paid Dr. Wrinkle so much money that when his son made his college valedictory speech he thanked *me* for making it all possible.

SEPTEMBER 5

Dear Diary:

Spent most of the day at the pool, lying on a chaise lounge, in a bathrobe, with cucumbers on my eyes. Not to help heal the stitches; I was being t-bagged by Melissa's greengrocer. That's one of the differences between New York and L.A. In New York when you order fresh vegetables, "fresh" means they're two days away from being part of a landfill on Staten Island.* In L.A., "fresh" means that the cleaning lady's husband's third cousin, Jacinto, who sleeps on a mat in their garage, is down the road picking them as we speak, and they'll be washed, cut and in my salad shooter before you can say "border patrol."

Speaking of vegetables, I hate it when people refer to paraplegics as "vegetables." The lack of specificity drives me crazy. What *kind* of vegetables? Tubers? Yams? Beetroots? It's not accurate to call Drooling Dave or Catatonic Cathy "vegetables." Vegetables are growing organisms; Dave and Cathy are end tables.

SEPTEMBER 6

Dear Diary:

Cooper starts school this week and he's at that age where he's going to start thinking about dating. I don't know if Melissa has had the birds-and-the-bees talk with him yet, but I hope she included surrogates, petri dishes and turkey basters in the conversation.

In my day it was so much easier. When I was a kid, getting to second base meant the girl let the boy feel her

---

* Just a note that on the East Coast a "landfill" is a term used by the Department of Sanitation when they refer to a garbage dump. On the West Coast, a "landfill" is a term used by the NBA when they refer to Kim Kardashian's uterus.

up. Nowadays it means she slept with half the Yankees' infield. All my mother ever told me about the facts of life was, "Joan, sex is easy. The man gets on top, the woman gets on the bottom." I bought bunk beds. I literally knew nothing. On my wedding night, I'd never seen a naked man before. When my husband, Edgar, came out of the bathroom, I hung my blouse on him. And I think those days were better. As I said to Melissa, "Your generation just bangs anything; it's wrong. Sex should be a beautiful thing that a woman shares only with the man she loves or, if he's out of town, her husband."

I worry that kids today are having sex so much earlier. It used to be that if you were a slut you'd be ashamed. Now girls put it on a resume.

And by the way, I hate the terms "baby daddy" and "baby mama." A baby daddy is just a horndog who was too cheap to buy a condom and a baby mama is the local slut who got knocked up in the back of a truck. You shouldn't be a "baby" anything if you're still wearing Pull-Ups yourself.

SEPTEMBER 7

Dear Diary:

Turns out it's not just kids who are getting whorier—older people are getting skanky, too. I was just at the mall (I don't shop in malls, I just like to sit in front of Abercrombie & Fitch stores and say to fat people who are thinking of going in, "Keep moving, Tubby, not for you. You need a sarong, just go to Bed Bath & Beyond."), when I saw a woman walking through the food court wearing a T-shirt that said, "Blow jobs are the new black." I was horrified. "Meryl," I said, "have some dignity. You're a star. Be a fucking lady."

SEPTEMBER 8

Dear Diary:

Back to New York for Fashion Week for *Fashion Police* and I'm a little depressed. There seem to be no rules anymore. I always believed in "No white 'til Memorial Day," but then you see a picture of the Pope. "Black is thinning," then you see a whale. And the rule "Don't overdress for church," and then Mother Teresa would show up for prayer meetings in a leper-skin jacket.

There's nothing quite like Fashion Week: hundreds of emaciated runway models staggering around, hoping they have the strength to live and pose another day. It's like *Schindler's List* with better clothes.

Fashion Week is a little bit of heaven: gorgeous clothes, great accessories and thousands and thousands and thousands of gay men . . . Normally if you want to see that many gay men in one place you have to look inside George Michael's mouth.

SEPTEMBER 9

Dear Diary:

Going to the Fashion Week Gala tonight. Can't wait. It will be all the beautiful people. And Mayim Bialik. I love going to the gala and people watching. My favorite thing to do is play a game I call "Make Anna Wintour Smile." The way it goes is, I sneak up to her table on all fours and tap her on the shoulder and say, "Psst, Anna . . . ," and then I show her pictures of bus plunges, sick puppies and orphans. Last year I actually got her to giggle when I showed her a video of a military funeral.

Another fun thing is taking bets on which cater waiter will snap first. All night long these poor boys walk around with full trays, getting more and more frustrated as the evening wears on because nobody will eat anything. Their arms get so tired 'cause the trays are getting heavier and heavier, and they start getting all pissy and snarky, and begin saying things to the models like, "Care for a grape, or will it make you look fat?" or "How about half a carrot? You can purge that up in no time flat," or, "Hey, Skeletora, why don't you have a parsley sprig? It'll help wash the vomit from your breath."

SEPTEMBER 10

Dear Diary:

Tonight was my first free night in two months and I was so looking forward to maybe just having a great dinner with friends, shoplifting with Winona Ryder at Walgreens, or just relaxing in Coney Island under the boardwalk under a sailor. But then I got a call from my florist's husband's adopted son from an earlier marriage, Peony Schwartz, inviting me to see a play he had written. PeePee is a nice guy and the ticket was free so I accepted.

I've heard of Off-Broadway, I've heard of near Broadway, I've heard of above Broadway, but if this theater were any farther from Broadway the play would be written in Swahili. And the "theater" itself is what Off-Broadway-ites call a black box—not to be confused with the device authorities look for when a plane goes down, or Kesha's vagina, although they probably have the same seating capacity. It's a little ninety-nine-seat room with a stage that's surrounded by three black walls. This means there will be very few props or lighting.

I was optimistic about the play, and rightfully so, as it turned out to be very interesting. It brought to light the real truth about Helen Keller's life. Yes, yes, yes, we all admire Helen but apparently she was boring. She had one story that she regaled her friends with over and over and over again: "I pueoro dniuwqq ce7393nd djeueuweueu snsf7483))dndj."* She was also very stubborn and insisted on driving, saying to her friends, "Efncjis wnx e7w12ncnc9qwjqm snshd7dqwjvcnui^b 48ssjsj."† And the play brings to light how everyone despised her

* I put my hand under the faucet and said my first word, "Wawa."

† I can drive; I'm not handicapped, I'm handi-capable.

equally deaf parrot, Mdhdyw.* Mdhdyw, instead of speaking, would scratch words with his sharp talons into Helen's friends' palms, causing them to bleed profusely and require a tetanus shot. What I liked best about the play was the title, which was so catchy: *Helen Keller, Shut the Fuck Up!*

SEPTEMBER 11

Dear Diary:

I woke up this morning and realized it was 9/11, one of my least favorite days because, out of respect, so many stores are closed. Being in New York on 9/11 is very difficult. The ceremonies and parades and dignitaries and politicians really fuck up the traffic. It took me almost an hour to get to my nail salon and I live only five blocks away. Believe me, *no one* is sorrier about the planes and towers and jumpers, but it's been well over a decade—can't we figure out a more efficient way to "remember" so I don't have to miss my appointment and walk around with the feet of a Japanese prisoner of war?

I feel *terribly sorry* for the families of the people who died on 9/11 in the planes and towers, but I feel even sorrier for the relatives of the people who just dropped dead naturally, or were in a car accident, or had a heart attack, or slipped in the tub, or were savagely bitten in the face by their unneutered male pit bull, Sugar. Their

* Polly.

families not only don't get any sympathy, they get scorn and ridicule thrown at them. If they even mention, "My husband died on 9/11," everyone just automatically says, "In Tower One or Two?" And then they have to say, "Neither. Albert had a stroke while eating a pretzel in front of a Best Buy on Queens Boulevard and . . ." They usually can't even finish their sentence as they've just been punched in the mouth.

SEPTEMBER 12

Dear Diary:

Just landed in Palm Springs to do a benefit for Barry Manilow, who lives there. Barry says he loves it because even though he's no chicken himself, he's definitely the youngest one in town. "Where else, Joanie," he says, "can a man over fifty be called 'boy' other than Birmingham, Alabama, or Cloris Leachman's bedroom?"

I love Palm Springs. It's often called the "gay nineties"—because other than the celebrities, half the people are either gay or ninety. It's the only place on earth where I can walk down the street and see old women who've had more plastic surgery than me, or middle-aged gay men who've had plastic surgery to look like me.

Performing at benefits can be tricky, especially if the infirmed, disabled, disfigured or famished I'm raising money for are in the front row. Try doing twenty minutes about flying coach in front of the Lockerbie survivors. That's a tough crowd. Forget laughter; they're so reconstructed they can't even move their mouths to boo—there's just a lot of guttural moaning. Sounds like Kathleen Turner's husband, when she's on top.

SEPTEMBER 13

Dear Diary:

I love Palm Springs and Barry is a wonderful host. The thread count on his linens is even higher than my age. He has pretty little soaps in the bathroom and fancy guest towels; they're perfectly ironed and arranged and I feel so guilty about using them, as I know Barry has spent hours ironing. But if I don't use them he'll think I'm a pig, so after a bath I waltz into the living room naked and dry myself on the drapes right in front of him. This way he knows I'm a fucking lady and I got taste and manners.

SEPTEMBER 14

Dear Diary:

Just got an invitation to a book signing for Paul Anka's new memoir. Paul Anka! I'm going because I don't want that little shrimp to be alone. Who's going to read it? His fan died in 1997.

SEPTEMBER 15

Dear Diary:

Back in L.A. Drove from Palm Springs last night. Anywhere else in the U.S. it would have been a two-hour drive. It took me over five hours on a four-lane freeway. Who are those people and where are they going? There's not that many interesting things to do in L.A.—you've seen one tar pit, you've seen them all. They say there will be six million more cars on this freeway by 2020, so if you need to cross it to get to Starbucks, do it now.

To make matters worse, I hated my driver. He talked from the moment I got in and never shut up. He knew who I was so he assumed I must know who he was, and that what he had to say about the Redskins, or the Blueskins, or the Purpleskins would intrigue me. He thought wrong. I can get Prince Charles, Woody Allen and Elton John on the phone—collect, if I use my Beyoncé voice, and say things like, "Stop that, Jay-Z, I don't like my nipples powdered when I'm talking to big-time people." And yet somehow Leon from Tarzana thought I'd find *him* intriguing, and be biting my nails and wetting myself as he bowled me over with stories of the heavy traffic flow on Sepulveda Boulevard. If I want to know about heavy flow, I'll watch Octomom change her tampon.

SEPTEMBER 16

Dear Diary:

Last night on the local news they did a story about some new KKK-like, white supremacist, neo-Nazi group in the L.A. area, and my first thought was, "OMG!! This is awful." Tomorrow morning every lawyer and agent in Hollywood is going to be storming City Hall . . . not to protest the hate group's presence in their neighborhood, but to change their names from Glickstein to McGlickstein. God forbid they should alienate the anti-Semitic demo and lose the chance to make a coupla deutsche marks on film distribution in Stuttgart.

I hate the term "white supremacist." First of all, it implies that these haters like *all* white people, and that's not true. I'm white. Harvey Fierstein is white. Some of Mariah Carey is white. I'm pretty sure they wouldn't like us. And my gay, albino rabbi agrees with me. And second, no way are these people "supreme." When your hood is made of faux percale and has a thread count of twenty, you're not a white supremacist; you're white trash.

SEPTEMBER 17

Dear Diary:

My old agent, Steve Levine, has set up a couple of pitch meetings for me at different networks. Some mainstream, some cable and some you can only get if you live in a glass house located where the 40th parallel bisects the International Date Line.

I hope one works out, and then maybe next summer Cooper won't have to go to South Africa to work in the diamond mines wearing pants without pockets.

Yes, dear diary, I worry about Cooper's future. From the start, I loved being a grandmother. It was wonderful to finally have something to bounce on my knees besides my boobs. And to this day, I am still hoping he will grow up to be a man of character, integrity and principle; in other words, someone who will never be president of the United States.

SEPTEMBER 18

Dear Diary:

I've come up with a couple of great show ideas to pitch to the networks. Yay me! I've been thinking . . . The creative people who run TV networks are lawyers and accountants who weren't creative enough to make it as lawyers or accountants, so they became television executives. They wouldn't know a good idea if it sat on their face, the way their twenty-year-old development girl/secretary/personal assistants do, so give them ideas they can understand. Don't pitch them anything original or groundbreaking. Pitch them new takes on old shows. So I decided to combine some hit shows that are already successful. For example:

1. *Tiny Stuffers*: I've combined *Little People, Big World* with *Hoarders*—families of dwarves who live in filthy dollhouses cluttered with footstools and stepladders. In the pilot, we visit tiny Grandma hoarder and find a dead Chihuahua blocking her driveway.
2. *Honey Boo Boo: SVU*: Two very good-looking detectives try to find out who had sex with Mama June, and rather than arresting him, they give him the Congressional Medal of Honor for getting it up.
3. *Larry King Sorta Live*: Larry hosts a call-in talk show on the days he isn't on life support or taking his meds. Every call starts with, "Hello, Forest Lawn . . ."
4. *Dancing with the Biggest Loser*: The cast of *The Biggest Loser* tries to win the dance competition. Watch the fun begin as we wait for Derek Hough's legs to buckle when he tries to dip Massive Mona. And Bruno says, "You are so light on your hooves for a morbidly obese, six-hundred-pound Guernsey cow! You go, Elsie!!!"

SEPTEMBER 19

Dear Diary:

I was supposed to go to Malibu to play tennis with Goldie Hawn but there was bad weather. (The waves were higher than Justin Bieber.) Everything cleared up at 11:30 and old Goldie's nurse called and said she'd like to try it. Goldie's one hundred and thirty years old and she still plays tennis—amazing. Turns out it's not the only game she's good at. She also plays "Where Are My Teeth?" "Do I Smell Funny?" and "How Come Grandpa Isn't Moving?" But give Goldie credit: It's hard to serve while in a scooter. I think she cheats a little; every time she fell down she'd use her "I've Fallen and Can't Get Up" buzzer.

SEPTEMBER 20

Dear Diary:

On the plane to do a one-nighter in Reno and I'm sitting right next to a hearing-impaired stroke victim. The moaning and slurring are very deafening and I can't tell if she's cumming, dying or asking for coffee. Being gracious, I smiled and said to her, "Yo, Droopy—what's your name?" She said Susan. Or Jill. Or Debbie. Or Brplmpjhuh. Turns out she's Chatty Cathy. We've been in the air for almost two hours and the bitch hasn't stopped groaning and yelping at me since takeoff. It's like being in a flying slaughterhouse. I'm going to offer the pilot twenty bucks to whisper the next safety announcements just to force her to clam up and listen.

I just looked at the term "slaughterhouse." Am I being too rough? Too on the nose? But maybe not. I like words that when you say them, you know exactly what's going on. Whorehouse. Vaginal itch. Ugly bride. You know where you stand.

I hate euphemisms. Like "powder room." It's a toilet. Yes, some women go in there to powder their noses. But more women go in there to take a shit. True, there are some women who go in there to powder their turds, but they're few and far between and they're usually makeup-artists-in-training or Danny Thomas's ex-girlfriends. (There's always been this urban legend that Danny Thomas liked to lie under a glass coffee table and have a hooker come over and take a dump on the table. He should have named his TV show *Make Room for Doody*. I don't believe this is true, but I've known his daughter Marlo for forty years and not once have I ever seen her wear brown.)

SEPTEMBER 21

Dear Diary:

The Danny Thomas urban myth got me to thinking about *other* Hollywood legends that may or may not be true:

RICHARD GERE, ANIMAL LOVER: For years rumors circulated about Richard Gere: first, that he was gay, and second, that he kept gerbils up his ass. (I never heard anyone say whether the gerbils were male or female.) I have no idea if Richard rented out his sphincter as a Habitrail but if he did, rather than mocking him as some kind of a freak, I preferred to think of him as an animal lover who saved rodents' lives by turning his poop chute into a no-kill shelter.

MICK JAGGER, CUM GUZZLER: As far back as I can remember (and with my oncoming dementia, by next month that may only be since 4 o'clock), there was a story going around that Mick Jagger wound up in an emergency room and the doctors pumped a gallon of semen out of his stomach. I'm not a math major but I'll bet swallowing a gallon of anything isn't easy, let alone semen. I have trouble believing this tale. Mick Jagger is a *very* busy man; he doesn't have the time to suck off the entire Mormon Tabernacle Choir.

MAMA CASS, HAM CHAMP: The rumor is that while in France, Mama Cass, of the famous rock group the Mamas & the Papas, choked to death on a ham sandwich. Her daughter, Daughter Cass, says that's not what happened. She said her mother died of natural causes. I say, if you weigh over eight hundred pounds, choking on a ham sandwich is a natural cause, but I'm not a doctor. All I do know is that the police report mentioned that Cass's room was littered with crumbs, mustard, hooves and a couple of pink snouts.

TOM CRUISE, GAY BLADE: Ever since Tom appeared in his underwear in *Risky Business*, people have been saying he's gay, but there's no actual proof to support the rumor. Just because a rich, handsome movie star who belongs to a creepy religious cult and travels the world with longtime male friends can't make his marriages work, it doesn't mean he's gay; it means he's fussy. And if you don't believe me, ask Kelly Preston.

SEPTEMBER 22

Dear Diary:

Back from Reno and had lunch at the Ivy with Smiling Steve Levine. Well, I didn't actually have lunch with him—he was having lunch with his more important clients, Andy Dick, Tito Jackson and the ShamWow guy, and I was waiting at the bar for a table out back behind the Dumpster to open up. The Ivy is a showbiz restaurant where coked-up, bulimic actresses meet their tweaked-out gay agents to grind their teeth and discuss business over scrambled egg whites they don't eat. While I was waiting, who should come sauntering in but Jon Hamm and a lady friend. According to the tabloids, Jon Hamm is hung like a horse. In fact, I've seen a nude picture of him from when he was in college and it looked like he had a child in his lap. They claim his schvantz is so big that when male horses talk among themselves they say things like, "I hear Flicka's hung like Jon Hamm." FYI, I'm not a size queen. In fact, I'm turned on by Chinese men. To this day, every time I'm in a delicatessen and I see an egg salad garnished with gherkin pickles, I start fantasizing about Jackie Chan.

SEPTEMBER 23

Dear Diary:

Red-eyed in to New York today and it's the first day of fall! Fall is my favorite season because as the temperatures cool down, the people smell less, and a ride on the subway is no longer like a week in a men's room. And for a brief period of time, maybe a week or ten days, the homeless suddenly look like fashionistas, wearing multiple layers not just at the right time, but slightly ahead of the rest of us. If I can get my agent to come to New York, I think I have a show for Bravo: *Project Bowery*, where we get the homeless to compete to see who can put on the most jackets and hats and pants at one time, without ever stopping to bathe or urinate indoors. Andy Cohen, here I come!

SEPTEMBER 25

Dear Diary:

According to the *Enquirer*, O. J. Simpson has put on a lot of weight and prison doctors are worried that he's getting depressed. I don't understand this. Why would he be depressed? The man doesn't have a care in the world. He no longer has the pressure of going on auditions or making mortgage payments or renewing his driver's license with the correct birthday or having to listen to his dumb lawyer, Johnnie Cochran, reciting bad poetry. I listened to him and Johnnie at lunch one day and Johnnie kept saying things like, "If the chicken don't smell, the cook can go to hell," and, "If Kato don't lie, you're gonna fry," and, "If I save your ass, I'll have money for gas." And most important, O. J. no longer has to listen to that slutty dead wife of his nag and nag and nag. So buck up, Juice—other than showering with "Big Ed" twice a week, your life is hunky-dory! All those people who say Disneyland is the "Happiest Place on Earth" have clearly never been to Cellblock 9 on a misty, moonlit April night.

SEPTEMBER 26

Dear Diary:

I didn't sleep at all last night, so now I'm tired and crabby and that's not good. Last time I felt like this I beat Pingpong within an inch of her life. I shouldn't say that; it's not completely true. I left her one hand unharmed so she could dust.

SEPTEMBER 27

Dear Diary:

Finally figured out why I've been so stressed-out and anxious recently. It's having to face the fact that I probably will not remarry, as all the age-appropriate single men that I know of are getting older or dying off. For example, I'm sad to say, a few months ago, Richard Ramirez—aka the Night Stalker—died in prison and I literally broke down thinking, "There goes a little piece of my past." In the 1980s, Big Dick, as I called him, terrorized Los Angeles and Southern California with a string of grisly murders of young, semi-attractive women. When they caught him I was both surprised and disappointed. Surprised that he wasn't even a little more attractive and disappointed because I realized that all the time I'd spent wandering around freeway exit ramps wearing frilly little dresses was for naught.

And now Charles Manson is starting to look his age, which I guess is understandable because he's seventy-eight. Seventy-eight! Wow, our little Chuckie, can you believe it? I saw a recent photo of him and I was quite shocked. In spite of his rather unhealthy lifestyle, he's always managed to stay spry and snappy, and even as his hair took on that sexy salt-and-pepper tone, he somehow maintained his impish manner. But now, all of a sudden, he looks jowly and sallow, and that maniacal stare that became his brand seems to have been lost to both time and a lazy eye. But the worst thing is, his skin is starting to sag and his forehead swastika is now under his nose, and he's starting to look like Hitler. And as a Jewish girl, I can't be having any of that.

SEPTEMBER 28

Dear Diary:

Flew back from a one-nighter in Boston and, my luck, I got a *very* pregnant woman sitting next to me, wearing a T-shirt that said, "I'm not fat, I'm pregnant." I had nothing to say to her, but to be nice I smiled and asked her the usual boring questions like: "Is it your first?" "When are you due?" "Have you picked a name?" Later it occurred to me that maybe there's a little niche business here: T-shirts for pregnant women that could actually move the conversation along. Wouldn't it be great if they could get something like, "Shit, the rubber ripped," or "I was tripping so I left my foam at home," or "The bastard said he would pull out," or "I'll do anything to get on *The Maury Povich Show*"?

Going to the theater tonight with my friend Margie. Not sure what we're going to see but as long as she's paying for the tickets it's fine. I'm happy to go to midget wrestling or a poetry jam or the execution of a retarded inmate, as long as it's free.

SEPTEMBER 29

Dear Diary:

Last night Margie and I ended up at this silly little Off-Broadway thing called *Naked Boys Singing!* Guess what it was about? You guessed it—naked boys singing songs about being naked boys singing songs. Not exactly *Death of a Salesman*, but in all fairness, I didn't get to see Willy Loman's penis swinging in front of me as he called for Biff and Happy.

One weird thing is that all of the men in the cast shaved off their body hair. All of it, I repeat, ALL OF IT. I find this very creepy, but Melissa says it's the new trend and almost all men are doing it these days. I can't imagine going out with a man who has no body hair; it would be like dating a giant nine-year-old. And unless you're Demi Moore, that's just wrong.

SEPTEMBER 30

Dear Diary:

Thirty days has September,
April, June and November.
All the rest have thirty-one,
Except February, which has twenty-eight except sometimes it has twenty-nine.
So leave me the fuck alone. I'm tired, I'm old and you're confusing me.

Whoever wrote that can't write poetry or do math and needs a near-death experience. I'm going to call my friends in the FBI and have them hunt him down and torture him—maybe send him to Attica or Guantánamo or make him go to a live taping of *Dr. Phil*. And I could do this; I have *lots* of friends in the FBI.*

* J. Edgar Hoover and I were very close. In fact, we were the same size. I used to lend him my clothes for special occasions. He looked especially fetching in a simple summer shift with matching cloche and open-toed shoes.

OCTOBER

If you think my tongue is big, you should see the size of the cold sore I gave Robin Thicke!

OCTOBER 1

Dear Diary:

I just got a call from my soon-to-be ex-friend Sylvia. She said, "Guess what? I just found out that on this date in 1962, Johnny Carson hosted his first *Tonight Show*." I said, "Guess what back? I don't give a fuck." Then I hung up and thought of calling my mob friends to see if she could "accidentally go swimming" in the Hudson River with something heavy in her purse, like John Goodman's lunch. I'm mad because she only told me half the facts. She never said that from then on Johnny was drunk and cheated on all of his wives.

And it's not just Sylvia who doesn't give the whole truth or all the facts. It's a blot on our society that our newspapers and magazines are filled with half facts and they never tell you the whole truths. For example, in April 1863, the first Siamese twins were separated, but it was never reported that in May their mother said, "I never would've done it if I knew that I'd have to pay for double *diaper service*." And I read that on October 1, 2009, paleontologists discovered the *Ardipithecus ramidus* skeleton, the oldest human fossil ever found. But what they didn't tell you was that while the fossil did not have a formal name, it answered to "Miss Dyan Cannon."

Half Facts Plus the Full Truth

HALF FACT: In 1776, George Washington crossed the Delaware and everyone declared him a hero.

FULL TRUTH: Fucking idiot was trying to get to Maine.

HALF FACT: The wettest spot on Earth is the Hawaiian island of Kauai.

FULL TRUTH: The second wettest spot on Earth is Cloris Leachman's Spanx.

HALF FACT: Infant beavers are called kittens.

FULL TRUTH: Adult beavers are called Mrs. Jodie Foster.

HALF FACT: An ounce of gold can be stretched into a wire fifty miles long.

FULL TRUTH: A pound of gold can be stretched into a never-ending alimony hearing.

HALF FACT: Swans are the only birds with penises.

FULL TRUTH: Black swans are the only birds with white girlfriends.

HALF FACT: In 2560 B.C., the great pyramids of Giza were finally finished using six thousand Jewish slaves.

FULL TRUTH: It should have been finished a whole year earlier, but the Jews took the winters off to go to Boca.

HALF FACT: The world's largest mammal, the blue whale, is known for weighing up to 150 tons.

FULL TRUTH: The world's second largest mammal is known for singing "R-E-S-P-E-C-T."

OCTOBER 2

Dear Diary:

I'm really pissed. I have very little time in New York but I spent the morning at FAO Schwarz looking to buy toys for my lesbian neighbors' new adopted twin girls. Some woman came over and asked me if I was their great-grandmother. *Great*-grandmother? Do I look that old? I would only accept that if I was from the Ozarks and I started birthin' babies at nine.*

This kills me that I look old!!! After all the money I've spent on Botox? And it's been *a lot* of money! Maybe I was wrong to do it; maybe I should have saved it just in case Cooper ever wants gender reassignment surgery.† Botox is not cheap and I've had a lot. Melissa says I've had more needles in me than a pine forest in Maine, and Cooper always adds, "Nana, you've been pulled tighter than Rick Santorum's asshole at a Pride parade."

---

* FYI, Miley Cyrus's mother is theoretically only fourteen years older than she, and Miley claims that she was a virgin until she was sixteen. Big deal. It's not that she was "good." She simply could outrun her brothers.

† I'm sure that Cooper will never want gender reassignment surgery, but one can hope. Why should Cher be the only entertainer to get years of free publicity for something she didn't have to lift a finger for?

And that cataract-riddled old crone thought *I* looked like a *great*-grandmother? I was so upset I went out to hire a PI to hunt down the old bag and push her under a Meals on Wheels delivery truck.

OCTOBER 3

Dear Diary:

Just came from visiting my lesbian neighbors. They're such a nice couple. I think their names are either Bonnie and Sue, or Connie and Rue, or Ellen and Portia, but it doesn't really matter; I call them Steve and Rocky and they always answer. They're both good-looking blondes from the Midwest (I think Steve was corn-fed; she's a rather strapping gal—thirty-six-inch inseam on her Dickies), but their new daughters look like Chairman Mao. They haven't picked names yet, but after looking at the babies and watching them gobble a lunch of green ferns and bamboo shoots, I suggested Ling Ling and Ding Ding in honor of the giant pandas.

OCTOBER 4

Dear Diary:

This is one embarrassed Jew. I had no idea that Depends leak. And if you don't believe me, ask the people sitting next to me on the breakfast dais at Temple Israel.

OCTOBER 5

Dear Diary:

I had two extra hours this morning so I laid in bed and tried to catch up on my essential reading. I like to be informed when I go to intellectual dinner parties (instead of being classified as just another pretty Hollywood blonde). The *National Enquirer*'s headline caught my eye immediately: Jessica Simpson says she's "found love and contentment with her womanly body." I studied her picture intently but couldn't tell if hers was a genuine happiness or a medicated happiness over weight gain, or if Jessica's just given up on dieting and no longer gives a shit. Her hips look so big that I'll bet she has to let out the shower curtain. Her idea of a wheat dish is Kansas. Anyhow, Jessica was smiling away and looking perfectly happy in her gravy-soaked muumuu that stuck to her now-pendulous breasts. This article made me angry. I hate big, fat celebrities who brag to the world, "I'm fat but I'm beautiful just the way I am." No, you're not. Everybody—and I mean everybody, including nice people, like Deepak Chopra, Marianne Williamson, and Billy, the forty-six-year-old box-boy who lives with his mother down the hall in #16F and still claps every time he makes a boom-boom—makes fun of you. That "I'm beautiful the way I am" kind of exaggeration gets me crazy. It's simply a justification to not do a sit-up, walk a block or have a salad. (By the way, I don't do sit-ups or walk a block or eat salads. It's not because I'm fat or lazy; it's just that I no longer have to. I have people to do that for me.)

I'm also sick and tired of people who actually buy self-help books and say, "I love me just the way I am." If you are one of these people, I want you to put *this* book down right now, strip naked and go and look in your mirror. Okay, are you looking? Don't you dare tell me you're glad you're you. If right now, you could trade your you for someone else's you, whose you would you pick? Here is a simple test that I would like you to take. Which would you prefer: A or B?

I Prefer:

A		B
My broken-out, oily blackheaded back.	OR	Angelina Jolie's silky, alabaster skin.
My flabby, cellulite-dimpled (not in a cute way) thighs; my batwing, Hadassah-hunk arms; my saggy, uneven, dark brown heavy-nippled breasts.	OR	A trim Japanese prison camp physique.
My fat, lumpy varicose veins.	OR	The smooth, rounded stumps of a heroic land-mine survivor.

If you have checked even one from column A, put down this book—I don't want to know you, speak to you or ever see you because you're crazy.

OCTOBER 6

Dear Diary:

What a weird business show business is. I saw in *TV Guide* that there's a special on TLC called *The Man with the 132-Pound Scrotum.* (Catchy title; I wonder what it's about.) This really was a one-hour show and I can't believe it—I know people in this business who spend their entire lives writing and studying and performing, and sadly, they often get nowhere, and now this slob gets his own special just because he has a ball sac the size of Cleveland? I'm trying to get in touch with him, to find his wife and then do a follow-up special, *The Woman with the Severely Crushed Pelvis.*

What upsets me even more are the names of television channels that no longer represent their product. A&E used to be "Arts & Entertainment," now they air *Duck Dynasty*—a show about hillbillies who shoot birds. Exactly which one of the arts is that? When was the last time you screamed "Bravo!" to a skanky, collagen-filled housewife from New Jersey?

And if you remember, TLC stood for "The Learning Channel." Please tell me what we're learning from this *132-Pound Scrotum* show? How he crosses his legs without crushing his nuts? How to make living room drapes into a Speedo? TLC has changed a lot—it used to be informative; these days it's all dwarves and midgets. TLC should now stand for "The Little Channel."

OCTOBER 7

Dear Diary:

Just read that Ellen DeGeneres is hosting the Oscars again. I wish they'd go back to the old days when they had comedians host the show.

I've decided my career is in the toilet. I'm an eighty-year-old heterosexual and the only drug I take is Boniva, so I might as well face it: I've got no shot at a big-time gig. As a matter of fact, my career is at such a low point that I'm writing this with the burnt end of a match in a bus terminal where I'm waiting for the 2:17 to Kalamazoo where I'm the opening act for a retrospective slide show on Tiny Tim. What did my parents do wrong?

OCTOBER 8

Dear Diary:

Lying in bed feeling very sorry for myself. On my way back from the club date in Kalamazoo the bus let me off on Kissena Boulevard to do a "personal appearance" in Queens. (A personal appearance is when a celebrity is paid to show up at an event and has to pretend that he or she cares about the people, the cause or the event itself.) I don't mind doing personal appearances for charities. As a matter of fact, every Christmas I do a benefit to raise money for gifts for lonely hookers whose johns are spending the holiday with their families. It's called Toys for Twats. I also am involved with a charity very similar to Meals on Wheels. We visit older men who take Viagra but are housebound. We just ring their doorbell and jerk them off. Ours is called Feels on Wheels. Anyway, I was at a banquet for some sick-kid thing and it was very upsetting. I thought, "This is so stupid. Why are they paying me when they could use this money for the sick kids?" It bothered me so much that I took all the money they gave me and did what any decent, empathetic person would do: went to Bergdorf and bought six Hermès bags. It made me feel better immediately.

Oh, I forgot to mention that as I was leaving the event, I heard lots of loud, terrible barking. My first thought was, "What's Susan Boyle doing in Queens?" but then I looked around and saw a couple of teenage boys walking pit bulls. At least I think they were pit bulls. I'm not sure as neither one of the dogs had a baby in its mouth. I said to thug-in-training number one, "Why do you have an unneutered male pit bull?" He said, "It's an attack dog." I said, "You live in Forest Hills. Not the Serengeti. Who's going to attack you, the Widow Feinstein?"

OCTOBER 9

Dear Diary:

Speaking of dogs, here is a sad afterthought: As I was going out, I met my neighbor carrying her little girl Fiona's dead puppy, Chuckles, all wrapped in newspaper. She was dumping Chuckles in the garbage and she was very upset, as she didn't know which bin to put the stiff, rotting corpse in—paper, plastic or recyclable. "I don't know what to do," she said. "He's dead and he's wrapped in paper, but his collar is plastic." "Easy peasy," I said. "The people next door are Korean. Put Chuckles in the recycling bin and call it a day; #18B does it all the time with semi-dead kittens." We spent the next couple of hours figuring out how to tell Fiona that Chuckles wasn't chuckling anymore. I told her about the way my parents broke the news to me when my best pal, my closest companion, whatshisname died. They took my favorite toy and ripped it to shreds. Then they called me and said, "Joan, Joan, look what your dog did!" I said, "Oh, oh, I wish he were dead." My mother smiled and said, "Good news, honey. He is!"

Unfortunately Fiona didn't have a favorite toy but she *did* have a brother no one in the neighborhood liked. No one's spotted Little Jimmy since 9 a.m.—and frankly, no one in the neighborhood cares. (He was unpopular and so ugly that he was even turned down at a petting zoo.)

Losing a pet is tough. A pet is one of the only two things in the world that give you unconditional love. The other being your vibrator. I've always been a big animal lover but only lately have I begun to appreciate cats. I always found them annoying and too aloof, always thinking they were better than I was, just like my cousin Bernice. But I'm coming around because I realize they make great fur coats (as the children of my cousin Bernice with her hairy ass will someday find out). As a child I remember telling my mother, "I hate cats; I hate cats." And she said, "Fine. Then eat around it."

OCTOBER 10

Dear Diary:

It's 11 p.m. and I just got home from a poetry reading at a hipster café in the Village called Café a-Go-Go, and after listening for an hour to bad poetry, I was upset that I hadn't left the Go-Go and Gone-Gone. Anything up to and including being stoned to death by angry rebels in Tahrir Square would be a lot more fun than listening to some Jesse Jackson wannabe complain about "The Man" in an ABAB rhyme.

"I hate you, mister, 'cause you fucked a sister." Yeah, yeah, boring—we heard it already on *Dr. Phil*.

Poetry is bullshit. For openers, all those rhyme-crazy morons—Yeats, John Donne, e.e. cummings and Wadsworth, just to name a few—were just fairy boys who sold a gullible public on the fact that poetry is terrific. Poetry is just stories being told in a short form by "poets," who are people who got rhyming dictionaries for their birthdays and who can't punctuate or write in complete sentences. Think about the "greatest poets" of all time—T. S. Eliot, Robert Frost, Carl Sandburg. If they were so great, how come you couldn't pick them out of a police lineup even if your life depended on it? I could pick out Gotti, and I could identify Larry King's testicles while blindfolded before I could tell the difference between the faces of Longfellow, Shakespeare and Emily Dickinson.*

* FYI, Emily was known to be a little mannish in her appearance because of the mustache, furrowed brow and Adam's apple. How times have changed. Hillary Clinton has the same characteristics and no one's calling her butch . . . to her face.

I'm going to bed. I need my beauty sleep. I plan to wake up in 2037.

OCTOBER 11

Dear Diary:

Went to visit my friend Flower, who recently moved to Brooklyn. Flower kept telling me, "Oh, Joan, you've *got* to come over; Brooklyn is the new New York." On my way to her house I saw three hookers, two rapists and a crack-whore pushing her kid in a baby stroller while the baby daddy rode shotgun. Flower is right.

OCTOBER 12

Dear Diary:

Just had my morning coffee and checked my calendar. It's Hugh Jackman's birthday and I don't know what to get him. It's hard to shop for very rich people because whatever they want they already have, or they can buy it themselves. Or worse yet, someone else will buy them a better, more expensive version of whatever I buy, and I'll have to smile and feign amusement, and then follow them home and kill them.

Hugh and I aren't "friends" friends; we don't hang out or go Rollerblading or carpool to bukkake parties; we usually just run into each other at movie openings or in restaurants, and he always comes over to me and says,

"Joan, you look beautiful tonight—for you." Then we exchange air-kisses and move on. I like Hugh Jackman; he can sing and dance and act, but the main, big reason I like him is because he's a survivor. In Nazi Germany, Elie Wiesel may have survived three years in Dachau, but in *Les Miz*, Hugh Jackman survived nine months filming with Anne Hathaway. THAT'S a hero.

Not one honest emotion ever comes out of Miss Anorexia 2013. After winning the Academy Award she looked directly into the camera and had the nerve to say, "I'm so happy tonight, I'm going to celebrate by eating a tomato *and* a baked potato." That's celebrating? It's like having an innocent man get out of prison after thirty-five years and to celebrate, the first woman he chooses to fuck is me.

I think I'll call Patti LuPone; maybe she can give me some tips as to what I should buy Hugh for his birthday. Be right back.

Later . . .

I'm back and Patti is brilliant. She said that since Hugh was "of the theater" I should get him something old and theatrical. So I went to Angela Lansbury's house and gift wrapped her. Actually, I went to the Drama Book Shop on Fortieth Street and got him a book. Their selection was great and I went back and forth between *How to Close a Show* by Sarah Brightman, *I Won't Fix My Teeth Even Though I Have the Money* by Andrew Lloyd Webber, and *Your Arms Are Too Short to Box with Anyone* by Kristin Chenoweth. Eventually I decided to buy Hugh a rare collector's item called *Famous Heterosexual Stage Actors*. It's only three pages long but it's riveting, I tell you.

OCTOBER 13

Dear Diary:

Hugh Jackman called. Said he *loved* the book, especially the foreword by Cary Grant. I love making people happy. I just hope someday I can make Melissa happy. Of course if I do, I won't be here to see it . . .

Off to QVC, and another opportunity to sell well-made dry goods and pretty shmatas to women in Iowa who have no idea what dry goods are or what "shmata" means. I love America.

OCTOBER 14

Dear Diary:

What a weird day. My former agent, Sensitive Steve Levine, called and said, "Get up, fatso. Margaret Cho just got sick and they're desperate for anybody so I think I can get it for you." It was a private party on a yacht for some rich Arab and his wives. This billionaire sheik (which I recently learned is pronounced "shake," so I now assume that Michael J. Fox suffers the "sheiks") was throwing a seventeenth birthday party for Wife #9, a petite, sloe-eyed girl from Abu Dhabi named Pashmasubraminium.

This club date was the worst experience of my life (if you don't count childbirth, conception, the closing of B. Altman's department store and that horrific poetry reading last Thursday). From the minute I got onstage to the minute I left, there was dead silence. They laughed at nothing. It was the worst show I've ever done and I'm not sure if it was me or if it was the Arabs, but in hindsight I'm pretty sure I shouldn't have opened with "Shabbat shalom." And my jokes about "How many Arabs does it take to change a lightbulb?" didn't go over well.* They stared at me the way Mohamed Atta stared at tall buildings. Live and learn. At least the check will clear because it was made out to "Jew Pig," so I know I won't have any trouble cashing it.

OCTOBER 15

Dear Diary:

On the plane back to L.A. I hate it when people carry on carry-on bags that are *so* big that they can't be carried on by a team of oxen. I'm sitting here in 2A, minding my business, silently passing judgment on the people heading to coach, when some schmuck comes waddling down the aisle dragging a steamer trunk that's big enough for either circus folk or Carnie Wilson's lunch. Unless he's carrying emergency medical

* None. They don't have opposable thumbs. Or: None. They don't have electricity in hovels. Or: None. They don't need electricity; they just set fire to an old wife, for light.

supplies or really good jewelry, there's no excuse for anyone to be that inconsiderate. Not only will there be no room in the overhead for other people's luggage, there'll be no room in the overhead for the bratty six-year-old in 4D, which is where I'm going to stuff that motherfucker if he doesn't stop whining.

OCTOBER 16

Dear Diary:

Took Cooper and his friends out for Mexican food tonight. I ordered a taco and Cooper and his friends ordered burritos, tortillas and quesadillas. Turns out all four dishes are made out of the same exact ingredients—meat, onions and cheese—they're just cut into different shapes. Mexican food is like bowel movements: Each one may look a little different but it's all the same shit.

OCTOBER 17

Dear Diary:

Valerie Harper was on *Dancing with the Stars*. Valerie has brain cancer and she goes on *Dancing with the Stars*? I'm in perfect health and can't get off the couch. What's wrong with this picture? I love Rhoda and along with the rest of America I'm so proud of her. I felt terrible when she had to withdraw halfway through her cha-cha because due to health reasons she could only cha. I truly pray she's still alive when this book comes out so she can sue me for every dime I have.

I've known Valerie for years and I truly like her a lot, but right now I'm jealous as hell. When Big Val announced she had terminal cancer she *immediately* got the covers of *People* magazine, *Us Weekly*, *Star* and the *Enquirer.* I hate that. I've had rickets, scurvy, cradle cap, rosacea and irritable bowel syndrome and I still have to go down on Anna Wintour just to get a below-the-fold blind item on page 178 of European *Vogue*.

OCTOBER 18

Dear Diary:

Very depressed. Still thinking about Valerie and her magazine covers. I just can't seem to get any free publicity these days. Michael Vick aced me out of the dog-beating stuff, Lance Armstrong owns the performing-while-under-major-drugs stuff, Helena Bonham Carter absolutely wins the ugly-with-talent award, and Amanda Bynes has a copyright on the mad-as-a-fucking-hatter matter. I'm pissed. I called my PR girl (and I use the term loosely; she hasn't seen a tampon in twenty years, not even to wash bottles with), Peggy Katz, and asked, "Why, why, why?" Peggy said, "Face it, thunder-thighs. You're not a compelling story. We milked the husband's suicide like an old cow with one teat left. Unless Melissa pushes you off a cliff we haven't got a compelling story."

OCTOBER 19

Dear Diary:

Just got finished watching the local news, which covered a freeway closing, an uncontrolled forest fire and the "compelling story" of an old man driving through a farmers' market killing sixteen innocent Japanese shoppers. At the end, while the reporter was in tears, the anchorman said, "Great job." I'm sick of anchormen saying "great job" to all the field reporters at the end of every report. A *great* job in journalism was Edward R. Murrow at the McCarthy hearings, or Walter Cronkite's coverage of the Vietnam War, or Woodward and Bernstein investigating Watergate. Pretty Pei Zei reporting on a broken sprinkler in the Galleria Mall is not a "great job" in journalism. It's a pretty Asian girl with shiny lip gloss *getting* a great job in journalism because she's screwing the assistant station manager who told her he's lonely because his wife is an invalid.

Also, everything is not "breaking news." 9/11 was breaking news. The BP oil spill in the Gulf was breaking news. Jackie Kennedy not wearing a wash-'n'-wear suit in Dallas was breaking news. A house fire in Malibu is not breaking news (unless a semi-important celebrity perishes in the blaze and can only be identified by dental charts or implant records); it's a real estate opportunity for Donald Trump.

OCTOBER 20

Dear Diary:

Going to Wisconsin to do a concert for the Annual Friends of Cheese Festival. This is one of my favorite gigs; the pay is great and there is nothing more challenging than trying to make fifteen hundred constipated people laugh without farting.

OCTOBER 21

Dear Diary:

Today is my dear friend Judge Judy's birthday. I was going to call her and sing "Happy Birthday," but I was afraid she would say, "Stop it! Was I looking at you? Who told you you were allowed to sing? Shut up until I give you permission!" I love Judge Judy, and the way she deals with people. She's like a three-year-old child because she always tells the truth and she doesn't edit. If Judy tells you you're an idiot, you're an idiot. I think she should be president. I'd vote for her. Over the past twenty years we've had Clinton, Bush and Obama: a hack, a quack and a black. I think it's time for a strong, tough leader. Want to stop all the nonsense in the Middle East? Screw the ambassadors! To hell with the diplomats and envoys! Fuck the Navy SEALs! If you want the fighting to stop, send over Judge Judy when she's in a bad mood. By the time she's done, Bibi, Achmed and

Mohameds one through twelve will be closer than Jerry Sandusky and the Boystown Glee Club.

OCTOBER 22

Dear Diary:

Another reason I love Judge Judy? She's worth $150 million. When I ask her if she wants to go on vacation with me to Tahiti, she never has to say, "Let me check my budget," because she owns Tahiti. She says, "Great. My treat; I'll have them clean it up for us. What color bananas do you like?" The only thing better than having a rich husband with three days to live is having a rich friend with an open wallet.

OCTOBER 23

Dear Diary:

Had dinner with two models at Le Cirque, one of the most expensive restaurants in the world. The bill only came to $26 and I had two entrées and pie. Those girls just don't eat. They smile and, like all anorexics, say, "I'm full from lunch." They forget to add that lunch was in 1997.

OCTOBER 24

Dear Diary:

I've spent the past two days obsessing about how rich Judge Judy is. Not that I'm the kind of petty, small person who's jealous of her friends. If any one of my friends is younger, taller, prettier, more successful than I, I wish them well. Dead, but well. I think about things like this a lot, when I'm in traffic or at the free clinic, but I don't worry about them. "Think" and "worry" are not synonyms. For example, if I'm in bed with a man, I don't worry if he's having a good time because I know he isn't. So what's the point of thinking that this will become a relationship and that maybe *he'll* stick around and pay for Cooper's medical school tuition, not to mention his graduation party and malpractice insurance? It ain't gonna happen; I'm lousy in bed. My vagina is so stretched out men ask me, "Is it in?" (Two years ago the Flying Wallendas walked across my vulva on a high wire with no help. The one major regret of my life is that if I had been with the Donner Party on that fateful day they could have found shelter in my uterus for the entire winter.)

OCTOBER 25

Dear Diary:

Busy day today. Did promos for all three of my shows: *Fashion Police*, *Joan & Melissa: Joan Knows Best?* and *In Bed with Joan*.

On my way home I saw something I've never seen before, and I don't mean Mama June having a salad. I usually walk down Fifty-Seventh Street to get home, but tonight I cut through Central Park because I wanted to save time and cop some killer weed. As I got to one of the transverses, sitting there on top of a fence post was an odd-looking creature with a huge head and giant eyes. I knew instantly it was either an owl or an Olsen twin. I went with "owl" because he didn't have a clothing line or an eating disorder.

In my lifetime, I've seen everything—vultures, rats, snakes . . . and that's just at Fox TV. But in all this time I never saw an owl. He just sat there staring, so I tried to get his attention by saying, "Hello, wise old owl," and by making little clicking sounds with my tongue, like a cicada or one of those African children we see in documentaries who are wildly happy even though they live in a hut and eat dust. The owl looked at me with eyes that contained centuries of knowledge, then spread his wings and soared majestically, smacking *pow!* right into a tree. He died. Dumb fuck.

OCTOBER 26

Dear Diary:

My friend Sue called me up this morning and asked me what my plans were. I told her I was going to the spa for a day of beauty. She said, "A day?!?! Dream on, sourtits, you need a week." What a cunt. That's why I like her.

While I was at the spa having my feet scrubbed and my thighs waxed, I was fiddling with my iPad and found this great website called Celebrity Net Worth which tells how much money actors, athletes, moguls and celebrities are worth. I found out that Paris Hilton is worth $100 million!!! At first I was really upset but then I realized that Paris Hilton might have a lot more money than I do, but I earned my money for what comes *out* of my mouth.

Barbra Streisand is worth $340 million, but I don't resent Babs because not only has she earned her money with talent and hard work, I know that every morning, right after she makes Jimmy Brolin bring her coffee and kiss her feet, she goes into the bathroom and has to look in the mirror.

OCTOBER 27

Dear Diary:

Went to a big New York City fund-raiser tonight and found myself sitting near former mayor Mike Bloomberg. I love Mike Bloomberg even though he's boring. (And he is boring. Prisoners at Guantánamo are offered the choice of waterboarding or listening to one of Bloomberg's State of the City speeches.) If Judge Judy decides not to run for president, then Bloomberg is my man. He's smart, he's rich and he's my height. That's a win-win-win.

OCTOBER 28

Dear Diary:

Flying back to L.A. today for a big *Fashion Police* meeting. I'm lobbying for more diversity in the selection of the celebrity photos we use. We like to use the hottest, hippest stars in town, but surely Rihanna can't be the only celebrity that regularly gets the shit kicked out of her by her man. Time to expand that demo! Get me pictures of other stars that got beaten up by their physically powerful significant others; get me Tina Turner; get me Halle Berry; get me David Gest. And if Tina or Halle or David are too old for our demographic, then maybe the ratings gods will shine upon us and someone will beat the hell out of a sweet, innocent Disney star, preferably one without a tail.

OCTOBER 29

Dear Diary:

Going to a German restaurant tonight with Melissa and my friends Peter and Larry. I go to German restaurants not because I like Wiener schnitzel but because I like to play a game called "Let's Upset the Goose-Stepping Waiter." We ask him questions like "Smells delicious; who's in the oven?" and "Does the chef cook with gas?" and "Is it Zyklon B?" These Nazis have no sense of humor. Only once in all the books I've read have I found a joke attributed to Hitler: "How many Jews does it take to change a lightbulb? None. They're all dead. Ha-ha-ha."

OCTOBER 30

Dear Diary:

Halloween is coming and it's my favorite holiday. It's also Miley Cyrus's favorite holiday. She just walks around the neighborhood ringing doorbells, posing and saying, "Trick?" Melissa, Cooper and I used to spend all day planning for Halloween, making costumes and buying candy and insulin. But lately costumes have changed so much. When I was a kid we'd dress up as ghosts or princesses or pirates. These are different times and nowadays kids' costumes are much more sophisticated. Cooper and his friends are going trick-or-treating dressed up as investors who were mildly affected by the Bernie Madoff scandal. They stand on doorsteps and burn black American Express cards.

OCTOBER 31

Dear Diary:

It's after midnight and I'm beat. Halloween is more exhausting than trying to stay in a conversation with Marlee Matlin. (How many times can you smile and say, "I hear ya', sister"?) First I went to the Halloween parade in West Hollywood, which is the gayest little town in America. Here Halloween is considered more important than D-day, Christmas or 9/11. Ten thousand gay men in drag on Santa Monica Boulevard . . . fabulous! I think of it as the Million Mary March. And even better, at least 4,621 of them were dressed as me, and only six as Tina Fey.

NOVEMBER

Condolences on your brother.

NOVEMBER 1

Dear Diary:

I'm sick and tired of getting e-mails from Pet & Pussy, my new pet store. Ever since I went in there myself a few months ago to buy food and treats for (the late) Max and Sam, Pet & Pussy and I have somehow become BFFs. I used to send Pingpong in to get my food and supplies, but when the dogs in the rescue-or-eat section saw her coming they'd begin to howl and yelp. They envisioned their ancestors being twirled on a spit or served up over a delicious, piping-hot plate of Asian noodles. Pet & Pussy e-mails me constantly. I hear from them more often than I hear from my lawyer, agent, manager and, of course, Melissa. I even hear from them more often than I hear from my plastic surgeon, and I hear from him a lot. ("Joanie, Dr. Frankenstein here. Saw you on *The View* yesterday and I must say, your left breast? Sag-a-rella! Call me!")

No one, and I mean *no one*, appreciates a sale the way I do, but Pet & Pussy is out of control. Unless you're Pamela Anderson, how many beef bones does one woman need? I may not be a pretty girl but enough is enough!

NOVEMBER 2

Dear Diary:

Went to a charming* hipster coffeehouse last night.

I hate coffeehouses with young, artsy types who wear torn clothes and funky hats and have scruffy beards and cracked feet. (And the men are dirty, too.) Listen up, people, "filthy" is not a style; it's a health problem. I don't consider soap or shampoo enemies of the state. If I want to sit next to something that stinks, I'll do a panel with Leno.

This unwashed, smelly trend started in Hollywood when Brad Pitt chose to leave both Jennifer Aniston and Camay behind. For some unknown reason this rich, handsome movie star decided that grooming and hygiene were beneath him and he wanted none of it.† Smell-a-rella Bradie Baby has been joined in the Pig Parade by fellow slobs Robert Pattinson, Colin Farrell and Johnny Depp. At least Bob, Colie and JD have an excuse: They're European. Well, at least Pattinson and Farrell are; Johnny Depp thinks he's French but in truth he's just a kid from Kentucky who majored in Dumpster diving. But it's not just men that are embracing fetid filthiness; there are plenty of young starlets stinking up the joint, too. Ever take a whiff of Courtney

* "Charming" is a euphemism for broken cups, sullen waiters and cockroaches.

† Shout-out to Brad: "Hey, Brad, if Rin Tin Tin and Lassie can lick their balls clean, so should you."

Love, or stand downwind from Patti Smith on a steamy summer day? They smell more than Ben Stiller's movies.

I've had thirty-six different noses in my lifetime and not one of them would survive more than a few minutes being locked alone in a windowless room with these stars.

NOVEMBER 3

Dear Diary:

Tonight I'm going to a hockey game with my Melissa. She wants me to "network." I'm not sure how a hockey game will help. If I want to spend time with men who have no teeth and fight a lot, I'll do a three-way with Bill Cosby and John McCain.

NOVEMBER 4

Dear Diary:

Very disappointed. Kathie Lee Gifford had called me all excited that they were having a giant sale on illegal cheap kitchen help. I spent all night on the computer browsing Craigslist and found nothing. Then I clicked on a section called "personals." I assumed it was a category designed specifically for me. I figured it would say, "Hi, Joan. We've found twelve kitchen workers in your area. All of them tunneled in from Chico and Guadalajara and will work for a buck an hour plus a tuna fish sandwich."

It turns out I was wrong. The only way personals involve illegal kitchen workers is if you're looking to finger fuck them between their shifts at the diner. Craigslist personals are for dating and hookups; kind of like a ChristianMingle but for people with genitals.

I couldn't believe how many categories there are:

m4w (men for women)
w4m (women for men)
m4m (men for men)
w4w (women for women)
wtf (men and women for Chaz Bono)

I think Craigslist should have a category just for me:

w4omwlomasea (woman for old man with lots of money and stage-eleven anything)

NOVEMBER 5

Dear Diary:

I am exhausted. I just got off the phone with my friend Jeffrey, who told me a long, boring story about how his little teacup Yorkie, Ox, saved his life. Jeff had collapsed during autoerotic asphyxiation and had a stroke three strokes away from completion. He was dangling from his shower rod when little Oxie came to the rescue. He barked and barked until some Good Samaritan broke in and cut Jeff down. And not only did the man cut him down, he also finished the job. Now that's *really* a Good Samaritan.

People are always talking about how smart their dogs are. "My collie, Ralph, kept a burglar at bay until I could call 911." "Our rescue greyhound, Tubby, pulled our drowning toddler out of a swimming pool." "Our Havanese, Sheila, knows when I'm blue, and runs and gets my slippers and licks my face." I never had this and I've had dogs all my life. I've loved them all, miss them all desperately, but in retrospect, they were all idiots. Here's a partial list of dogs I've loved and the dumb things they did:

BUNTY: A gorgeous big-eyed cocker spaniel; so dumb he once dragged a child *into* a burning building.

ANGUS: A feisty Welsh terrier; so dumb he used to drink right out of the toilet—when I was on it.

KING: A golden-coated boxer; he was both dumb and lazy. He chased parked cars.

WHIST: A very tall Airedale who was much bigger than all the other dogs in her litter. She never knew her name; she only answered to Khloé.

SPARKY: A cutie-pie Lhasa Apso who not only breathed very heavily like Rebel Wilson at a Dunkin' Donuts but was so dumb she spent hours trying to flush the fire hydrant.

TIGER & SHASTA: Two regal, strong German shepherds that were totally anti-Semitic. They were so dumb they didn't care that I was Jewish, and during Passover they'd constantly try to push the brisket back into the oven, along with my aunt Ida, who was holding the pan.

CALLIE: A gorgeous chocolate Lab. So lazy that she was really just a coffee table with paws and so dumb she spent her entire life sniffing butts and never got even one good movie role out of it, just like Courteney Cox.

SPIKE: My darling Yorkie. So dumb he spent hours humping Heather Mills's leg while it was still in the closet.

VERONICA: Another wonderful Yorkie. She was a lesbian but so dumb she mated with male dogs, and afterwards would growl at them, "Fooled ya!"

LULU: A sensitive Boston terrier. She only had three legs. Twice a day I had to take her out for a drag. She was so dumb that when I said "heel" she'd bite the back of my foot.

NOVEMBER 6

Dear Diary:

The holiday season is in full swing and there's no better time to be in New York City. Today the picture windows went up at Bergdorf and Saks, and as I walked down

Fifth Avenue in the crisp autumn air, it did my heart good to watch the homeless looking at those windows, knowing they're thinking, "Someday maybe I can live in a box in front of these fine stores." Hope is a beautiful thing.

NOVEMBER 7

Dear Diary:

THIS was in front of me on line at Starbucks today.

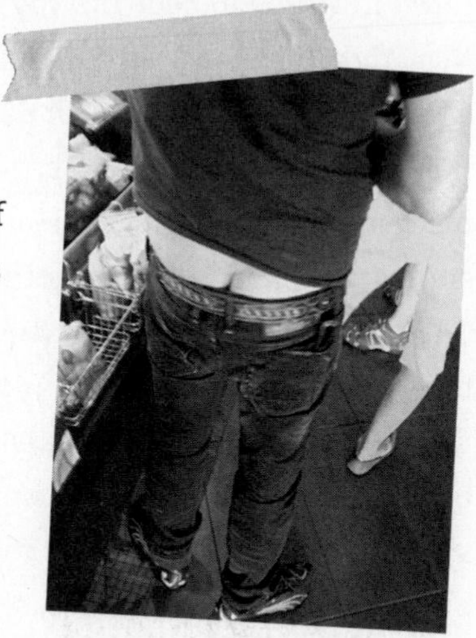

People are pigs. This is disgusting. How can any self-respecting human wear white pedal pushers in November?

NOVEMBER 8

Dear Diary:

I saw Debby Boone on TV tonight hawking a procedure called Lifestyle Lift, which is some kind of budget plastic surgery thing. I loved Debby and her greatest hit, "You Light Up My Life."

Truth be told, even though I loved "You Light Up My Life," I didn't love it nearly as much as Ted Bundy did. Ted and the electric chair operator at the Florida State Prison thought of it as "their song."

NOVEMBER 9

Dear Diary:

It's Sunday morning and I have the entire day off! I worked Friday and Saturday nights doing concerts and now I'm sitting in bed with my morning coffee and the *New York Times*, trying to figure out how to hide my weekend earnings from both the IRS and Pingpong. The IRS isn't too hard to fool,* but Pingpong is one crafty motherfucker, or as her ancient mother who she totally supports calls her, "clafty mothelfuckel." Case in point: The morning after last Thanksgiving, when I was going through the kitchen drawers counting all of the silverware, teacups and gravy boats, I noticed that a turkey baster was missing. I knew none of my guests would steal it, as I would never be friends with people who have to cook for themselves, so it had to be Pingpong, who was in charge of the holiday cleanup. I can't prove she took the baster, but when I barged into her little windowless attic room to confront her, through the gloom I saw Pingpong lying in bed, spent, smoking a cigarette and singing a blowsy rendition of "Build Me Up Buttercup."

* Last year on my tax return, I took $225,000 off for makeup. The IRS called me down, took one look at me and okayed it.

NOVEMBER 10

Dear Diary:

Flying back to L.A. today and got buzzed when I went through security. The TSA agents were going to wave me through but I demanded a pat down. I love pat downs. I just close my eyes and fantasize it's Ellen DeGeneres giving me a good feel. Anyhow, the reason I'm rushing back is because I got Cooper an audition to be the new love interest on *Keeping Up with the Kardashians*. Obviously he won't be with the regulars, Khloé and Kourtney and Kim and Kylie and Kendall, but just like that house in Cleveland he'll be with the new crop of Kardashians that are being kept in the basement. I know of Klunky, Kunty, Kryptonite and, my favorite, the baby of the group, Kreplach. There may be more I don't know; I hear Kris Jenner kept eggs in the freezer, so unless there's a major blackout and she turns them into an omelet, she'll Keep Kardashians Koming. I'm sure Cooper'll do fine; he's cute, charming, smart, athletic—he's a natural. The only negative thing is he might have to change his name to Leroy.

NOVEMBER 11

Dear Diary:

Just got back from doing a benefit for underprivileged children and you know what? Underprivileged children are damn exhausting. There are so goddamned many of them, and it's always the same story: a poor urchin, abandoned by a junkie mother, living in a shelter, eating the crust off his bunkmate's underwear because McLoser House doesn't have funds for fresh bread and pâté, blah, blah, blah . . .

I was happy to help out and raise a couple of bucks for Skinny Minnie and Boney Bobby, but I think these little pleading suck-ups would be able to make a lot more money if they learned to sing and dance and deliver catty asides, like the sore-covered orphans in *Oliver!* No matter how hungry or filthy or lice-ridden those kids were, they were never too down that they couldn't pull themselves up from the brink of despair and burst into a rousing chorus of "Consider Yourself." And you know what? *Oliver!* made $88 million at the box office worldwide, that's what. Which is a lot more than you can make being an old hag like me who comes in and tells cunt jokes for thirty-five minutes.

NOVEMBER 12

Dear Diary:

Woke up at four in the morning thinking about those underprivileged kids. Something was bothering me. There are hundreds of charities and government programs for underprivileged children, but none for *semiprivileged* children. And frankly, I feel *they're* the ones who need our help and support.

Poor kids never feel out of place; they fit right in with all the other poor kids. Poor kids don't ostracize and bully each other. Hobo-boy #1 doesn't make fun of Hobo-boy #2 because #2's rags aren't as smelly as everyone else's. Poor children are like communists: They're all the same and they seem to have found a happy comfort in the youthful common bonds of crippling poverty and bad hygiene.

The way I see it, it's the upper-middle-class kids that have a tough road to hoe. They're not poor so they can't talk about eating gruel or bringing cockroach sandwiches to school, but they're not rich so they can't join conversations about how sad it was when Uncle Bernie Madoff went to jail or that Aunt Imelda lost her entire shoe collection "when the commies took over."

Semiprivileged kids are the ones who face a shitstorm of derision when they show up at the country club that their parents can't really afford in a Honda CR-V, or are carrying a Gucci bag that even a minor trust-fund kid with glaucoma can tell they bought on Overstock.com, or, worst of all, have the faint scent of a domestic boxed wine on their breath. Welfare kids don't have to deal with the agonizing problem of finding the correct wine to go with their government cheese. Such esteem-crushing moments do however affect Debbie Debutante. Debbie, who's a cutter to begin with, would surely be driven to slashing if she knew that the other members of her parents' restricted country club found out that her kitchen staff was not only *not* live-in, but only part-time. I'm going to talk to my lawyer Gary Gonif about setting up a foundation to help these children break the glass ceiling and move into the privileged class, where they can look down on others without having the paralyzing fear of being looked down on themselves.

NOVEMBER 13

Dear Diary:

Really tired. Filmed three segments of my Internet talk show, *In Bed with Joan*. Doing three separate interviews is exhausting. Next week I hope they book Sybil. I can do sixteen different interviews with the same person and never have to change wardrobe or leave the bed.

NOVEMBER 14

Dear Diary:

Created a scene at the Ivy today. I was having lunch with Smarty Steve Levine (he's trying to get me an endorsement deal to be the Face of Colitis*), and who should sit down next to us but Ellen DeGeneres and

* Super Steve Levine did his job. As of January 1, I'll get $50,000 and two-ply toilet paper for life (I rash easily). I'm so happy. You can't see me now, but I've got a shit-eating grin on my face.

Portia de Rossi. Everything was going fine until Ellen and Portia both ordered fish. I started laughing uncontrollably. Ellen said, "Why are you laughing? Is it something I said?" I replied, "What are the odds on that one?" Ellen acted like she'd never heard this before and got all huffy and upset, and moved to another table, where she and Portia were soon joined by Dane Cook. They started talking and I stopped laughing immediately. Steve said to me, "Joan, as my thirty-seventh most important client, let me offer you a bit of advice. Do something nice to smooth this over. Ellen has a big talk show and you never know when you'll need her." So I said, "Okay," and I went into the kitchen and bought six jars of tartar sauce from the "French" sous chef, Jose. On my way out I stopped at Ellen's table and gave the jars to her and Portia. She said, "Oh, Joan, that's so sweet of you. Is this for our kitchen?" I said, "No, your bedroom." Steve said, "You'll never get booked; better call Latifah."

NOVEMBER 15

Dear Diary:

Watched TV with Cooper last night. Coop and I argued a little over what to watch. We eventually compromised and watched reruns of *The View*. (I miss the good old days of *The View*, when Barbara hated Star, Star hated Joy, Joy hated Elisabeth, and Elisabeth would hold up pictures of Hitler and discuss his good points: "He was a great dancer and never had to diet." Now *that* was good television.)

NOVEMBER 16

Dear Diary:

Trying to diet, but it's so hard. I'll eat anything. I floss with fettuccine. My friends in California say I should increase the fiber in my diet. So when I finish writing this diary, I plan to eat it.

Here's how I know it's time to diet:

- I stepped on a scale and it said, "Come back when you're alone."
- Last night I ate what I thought was a potato chip and two minutes later Cooper came in screaming, "Where's my turtle?"
- If I want to shed ten pounds fast, I drop my cat.

I've tried different diets, like the Rihanna diet. You date Chris Brown and he slaps the pounds off of you.

I love the Jewish American Princess diet. You never swallow. Then there's the Hollywood Starlet diet: Nothing goes in your mouth unless there's money involved.

I know, I know, diets just don't work. I have to change the way I eat. The only woman who ever lost twenty pounds and kept it off was Marie Antoinette.

NOVEMBER 17

Dear Diary:

As I am having lunch today with Matt Lauer, I tried to catch up on the important news of the day by reading *People*, *Us Weekly*, *TV Guide* and *Tiger Beat*. I accidentally picked up the *New York Times*—and I mean accidentally; the headlines were all about Cyria. Frankly, I don't give a shit about Ciria. It bores me so much I'm not even sure how to spell Syrya. It's not like *Fashion Police* is big in Damascus (there are only so many ways to accessorize a burka), and amidst the dull, useless stories about government budgets, Wall Street offerings and world famine, was a full-page ad that said, "Meeting Temple Grandin Is an Experience!" A woman who's studying library science at Texas Christian University wrote the ad.

First of all, anyone who majors in library science is in major trouble. Libraries are over. Whispering is not a science. Show me where there's a ground-breaking for a library that doesn't have a president's name on it and a gift shop in the lobby. No one goes to the library anymore except to buy Christmas gifts for people they hate: Nothing like giving people you hate decks of cards with drawings of famous literary giants on the back—Wordsworth, Sandburg, Whitman . . . Nothing says "Merry Christmas" like a two of clubs with Sylvia Plath's head in the oven on the back.

Face it, we don't need libraries; we have the Internet. Libraries are as over as Tony Orlando, with or without

Dawn, and this kills me, as I'll miss the guys masturbating in the stacks, and the sound of people ripping out pages that they planned to copy for their term papers.

Back to the Temple Grandin ad. What kind of an "experience" could it be meeting Temple Grandin? She looks like a deranged, middle-aged cowgirl with few social skills and mild flapping issues. Never mind "experience," I think the ad should be more specific, like "Meet Temple Grandin. Watch her ignore you as she rocks back and forth and beats her head on a wall while she eats her cereal."

FYI, some people say Temple Grandin should fix her teeth. I say, why? It's not like she's husband hunting. I say, "As long as they can chop, leave them alone."

NOVEMBER 18

Dear Diary:

Landmark New York buildings are like beautiful old ladies—and like most old ladies they have an ugly asshole. I live in a landmark building and, boy, does it have a huge asshole. She lives two flights above me and she's a deadbeat and a troublemaker and these are just her good points. She's the world's worst neighbor. Living next to the Unabomber, Ted Kaczynski, would have been better; other than the urine smell and occasional ticking from inside his shack, I hear that Teddy was a relatively pleasant fella.

Anyhow, she owes the building $200,000 in condo fees and the board is trying to get her out, but New York City's housing laws are so tight it was easier getting those thirty-three Chilean miners out of the ground than it will be to get this bitch out of her apartment.

NOVEMBER 19

Dear Diary:

Got a new dog! Just like Britney Spears, he's a rescue dog. He was found wandering around Lake Tahoe, looking for food, shelter and street-grade crystal meth. He's a Japanese Chin. He came home last night and he fit in immediately; I'm sure he's gay. Instead of humping my leg, he measured it and suggested I lengthen my hem and not be locked into black for a leash as my go-to color.

NOVEMBER 20

Dear Diary:

I'm starting to prepare for my big Thanksgiving dinner. It's my favorite holiday. Thanksgiving is a time to be grateful. Every year I throw a big catered dinner for family, friends and people who can either advance my career or destroy those of my competitors.

The hard part is the seating chart. Some people are

fascinating, some people are engaging and some are so boring that even if they accidentally brushed up against a candle and set themselves on fire they couldn't hold your attention. When I first started having these holiday dinners I combined the groups and mixed the fascinatos in with the dullos, thinking that each part of the table would have at least one interesting person sitting in it. I no longer do this. I sit all the bores together because it turns out bores don't know they're boring, which explains how Dr. Phil and Ann Curry seem to have so much fun interviewing each other while all of their viewers are slipping into a coma.

NOVEMBER 21

Dear Diary:

I love my new dog, but I hate his name. It's Teegan. Sounds like a drunken Irishman. If I wanted a dog named after a drunken Irishman I'd call him Colin Farrell. I'd like to change his name but he answers to Teegan and I don't know how long it would take for him to adapt to a new name. It took my cousin Shirley years to adapt to her new name, Elliott. It took him longer to adapt to the name than to the sex change. For years, if we wanted any response out of him we had to say, "Elliott! Shirley! One of you! Zip up your pants, your schlong is showing."

The only celebrity dog I know who changed his name was Rin Tin Tin. He was born Randy Tinowitz but he thought it sounded too Jewish for the business so he changed it. History will attest it worked like a charm and Little Rinny worked till the day he died. He even has a star on the Hollywood Walk of Fame! Six-pointed, but still, as I said to my rabbi the other day, a star's a star!

NOVEMBER 22

Dear Diary:

Today is the fiftieth anniversary of the assassination of President Kennedy, and all the postmenopausal women and residents of nursing homes are talking about is where he or she was when Kennedy was shot. I remember that morning like it was yesterday. Hard to believe, but I was in a coffee shop in Dallas, Texas, having breakfast with Lee Harvey Oswald! I had met him at an NRA breakfast. (Guess what the menu was? Bangers and mash!) He shot me a sexy look—actually he shot me three sexy looks in less than 4.9 seconds. How'd he do it? We clicked immediately. We found we both loved travel, books, suppositories and depositories (ha-ha) and felt pink tweed was wrong for November. Lee's first words to me were, "Don't Cubans make you laugh?" That morning we were making small talk (how to mow grassy knolls) when suddenly he jumped up and said, "Joanie, baby, I gotta run." I said, "Leelee, where to?" He replied, "I've got a thing downtown, and then maybe an afternoon movie." Then he took off and the rest is history. Now, all these years later, knowing what I know, when I reflect back on that fateful day, I *still* cannot believe what happened. That bastard. That sonuvabitch. That motherfucker. He left me with the check!

NOVEMBER 23

Dear Diary:

Going to the dentist today. Nothing wrong with my teeth, but at my age it's the only chance I get for a man to tell me to "open wide."

NOVEMBER 24

Dear Diary:

It's holiday season so I have to start getting my credit cards ready. Chanukah starts in three days, which is a huge pain in the ass because holiday sales don't usually start until *after* Thanksgiving. The Jewish holidays work off the Hebrew calendar, which is very confusing. They're just like the hip-breaking grannies in the Mt. Hebron Nursing Home—they fall at different times.

NOVEMBER 25

Dear Diary:

Off to QVC to hawk my baubles, bangles and beads. I love having my own line and I love being on QVC. But the TV pitchperson field is getting too crowded. At first there were just a few schmatte mongers on TV, but now every big star, minor celebrity and desperate has-been is on TV selling something. My favorite is Suzanne Somers. Suzanne fascinates me because there's nothing she can't and doesn't sell, and there's nothing she's not an expert on. If you want smooth thighs, fun recipes, tips on aging or cures for cancer, hunger and AIDS, Suzanne's your gal. Who would've thunk that Chrissy from *Three's Company* would become the Einstein of her generation? I'm so jealous of her energy; she makes Martha Stewart look like a paraplegic who mixes her cakes with a spoon held in her mouth.

NOVEMBER 26

Dear Diary:

Went out to dinner tonight with a couple of my theater friends (and when I say "theater friends" I mean two old queens whose scrotums are so wrinkled and brown you want to serve them with sour cream). We wound up sitting at a table near P. Diddy. We'd never met so I wasn't sure whether to call him Diddy, Mr.

Diddy, P, or PP. I walked right over to him and said, "What do I call you? Puffy? Puff Daddy? I'm Jew-Mommy."

I'm confused. So many rappers have nicknames, like P. Diddy and T.I. and Ray J, but those stupid nicknames really help sell records. I'm going to call my BFF Celine Dion and tell her she could hit the charts again if she gave herself a rap name. Knowing Celine, I'm going to suggest C. Unty.

NOVEMBER 27

Dear Diary:

Tomorrow is Thanksgiving and Cooper asked me who I liked better, the Pilgrims or the Indians. No contest. The Pilgrims. No disrespect to the Indians (and notice I call them Indians, even though I should be politically correct and call them Native Americans or Previous Owners)—if not for them I'd be broke and Cooper would be having Thanksgiving dinner at a bus station with a couple of hobos and Wesley Snipes.

I play a lot of Indian casinos and every day I thank God General Custer was a bad shot and left a few of those Red Fellows* alive, or I'd be broke. (I make a lot of wampum off of them.) Not once in all these years have I been hired to play a Pilgrim casino. But for me, if I had

* Capitalized, out of respect.

to choose, as I said, it would be the Pilgrims. You see, fashion trumps fairness and even though the Pilgrims stampeded and marauded the Indians, Cochise and his idiot pals *always* wore flats—not a good look for formal events or red carpets—and the two biggest Indian exports, blankets and turquoise, have zero market value on QVC.

The Pilgrims on the other hand are an absolutely untapped gold mine. When since Plymouth Rock, other than in costume dramas or on *Sister Wives*, have you ever seen a non-retarded person wear buckle shoes? Never! Even Payless doesn't carry them, and they sell footwear made out of cardboard and luncheon meat. I look at Pilgrim-wear as a whole new division of the Joan Rivers line. In fact, I'm going to call my designer first thing Monday morning and have him start working on buckles, aprons, ill-fitting black hats and dowdy bonnets. I don't care if Halle Berry herself wore them, they make any wearer unfuckable, and I think there is a huge untapped market for People Who Want to Look Unfuckable: Muslim women during Ramadan, girls who date rich lepers, and Jewish wives who have just had their hair done.

NOVEMBER 28

Dear Diary:

Don't have much time to write. It's Thanksgiving and I barely have time today to get a massage, do my hair, put on makeup, get a brow lift and microchip all the help before my relatives and hangers-on arrive. Bon appétit. Or should I say, knowing the guest list, gobble-gobble?

NOVEMBER 29

Dear Diary:

Last night was a huge success. The table looked beautiful, the food was delicious and my recipe for braised parakeet eyeball was a big hit, until they found out it wasn't caviar they were spooning onto their crackers. The highlight of my Thanksgiving dinner is always at the end of the meal when we go around the table and everyone gets up and says what they're thankful for. Most people mention their families or friends or health. Last night my favorite was when Jon Hamm's ex-girlfriend stood up and said she was grateful for padded chairs and vaginal rejuvenation surgery. Perfect end to a perfect evening.

NOVEMBER 30

Dear Diary:

I am still feeling so stuffed and bloated and huge from that great Thanksgiving dinner, so I'm spending the entire day today in bed, watching movies. I'm going to watch *Precious*, *Fatso* and *What's Eating Gilbert Grape*. I should feel better about myself in the morning.

DECEMBER

Why a Christmas tree? Because you can't fit a really big present under a menorah, that's why. And that's what the holiday season is all about.

DECEMBER 1

Dear Diary:

Today is Cooper's birthday! And I'm so proud of him. He's smart, athletic, a damn good student, and Melissa's smacked enough manners into him that people tell me he's very polite. He calls me Miss Rivers or Your Highness even when I don't make him. Kids grow up so fast these days. One day it's Slurpees, the next day it's herpes.

Today is also the anniversary of the day in 1955 when Rosa Parks refused to get off of a public bus in Alabama. She said, "You'll have to kill me before I get off one of these things." It's also the anniversary of the day in 1995 when Donatella Versace refused to get on a public bus in Milan and said, "You'll have to kill me before I get *on* one of these things." So all in all, December 1 was a good day for black-skinned women who make a difference and like to travel.

DECEMBER 2

Dear Diary:

I'm sitting on a plane to L.A. and someone is farting or decomposing. I know it's not me, as I didn't eat at Applebee's last week. Also, I'm in the first row and the smell is coming from behind me, and even though after all that plastic surgery my eyes are actually in the back of my head, my current nose is still sort of in the front, and I can't tell who the offending ass belongs to. The cabin is full and there are a lot of international passengers, so it might not be a fart at all; it might just be the BO of some rich French person who, while educated and well-off, has somehow not figured out how to work a shower. (Notice I didn't say "Germans" because if there's one thing Germans know how to work, it's a shower.) My eyes are watering and my nose is running; the cabin is like a sulphur mine with peanuts. Two more ass-blasts from Bad Salmon Betty behind me and the masks are going to drop from the ceiling.

DECEMBER 3

Dear Diary:

It was a cold, snowy day but Melissa's neighbors Brett and Marion managed to pay a visit and brought their brand-new baby boy, little Bretarion, along.* Over coffee and chocolate cake (the only thing Melissa serves in her

* I hate couples who take their names and combine them when they're naming their child. Sometimes it works, like Dee and Ann had a darling little girl named Deanne. But most of the time it doesn't. Jewel and Derek were obviously drinking when they cut the umbilical cord and named their little girl Jerk. (It could have been worse; they could have named her Jew-e.) Tyrone and Kitty made a huge mistake when they named their bouncing baby boy Titty. But the saddest case I've heard was when two very dear Chinese friends of mine, Fiona and Chuck Yu, took their darling little Fuck to Disneyland where they were physically ejected when they called out the baby's full name in front of Mickey Mouse.

house because it doesn't show the dirt), the couple began arguing over whether or not to circumcise him. Brett is Catholic and Marion is Jewish but *she's* the one who doesn't want to snip Bretarion's little schmeckle. She's one of those phony feminists who believes that circumcision is "barbaric" and "traumatizing" to the child. This is not so. Ask any boy who was circumcised as an infant. He doesn't remember it. But if you ask the one kid who wasn't circumcised, he remembers being teased in school, made fun of in the locker room and pointed at by pediatricians' evil nurses. Any prison psychiatrist will tell you that this is why, years later, he went back to his old school and opened fire in the cafeteria with an AK-47. A snip in time saves nine.

You want trauma? Talk to the women who've had to deal with a man's uncut monstrosity. Even in Europe, where anything goes, you never hear Inga or Ermgard say, "Oh, my Wilhelm has such a gorgeous schvantz! I love ze way his foreskin drags on ze floor and picks up crumbs and schmutz and dust mites." Personally, I have only seen an adult foreskin once but, because of this, to this day I am unable to go to the zoo or watch Animal Planet specials on elephants, tapirs or aardvarks. Even worse, I can't even look at an evening gown that pools on the floor without getting nauseous and weepy.

DECEMBER 4

Dear Diary:

Today I got a letter asking me to contribute to a charity for dwarves. I tossed the reply envelope away. I hate these little whiners. They don't know how lucky they have it. They don't have to worry about smoking stunting their growth. They don't have to worry about the wear and tear on their trousers' knees as they perform oral sex standing up. And if one of them gets shitfaced drunk and falls down in the gutter, he won't hurt himself because it's such a short drop. How much damage could you do from seven inches up? It's not like he's jumping off of Tower One. Talk about a win-win.

DECEMBER 5

Dear Diary:

I'm starting to put together my Christmas shopping list, which is not an easy thing. I have so many different types of people to shop for: family, friends (close, not so close and people I've been stuck with either by death, divorce or court order), A-list celebrities I know, A-list celebrities I'd like to know, publicists of A-list celebrities I'd like to know, network executives and their wives, mistresses and "pool boys," and anyone who has access to my medical records, financial statements or sex tapes. That's some list and it doesn't even include the people I hate.

I'm not a good gift-giver. Actually I'm not a gift-giver at all. Frankly, Scarlett, I don't give a fuck. I hate spending a nickel on anyone but me. Yeah, yeah, Christmas may be Jesus's birthday, but the party invitation Mary sent to me must've blown off the porch.

I have found that by not giving gifts, there are certain phrases you're guaranteed to never hear coming from my lips on Christmas Day:

- "I saw this at Goodwill and just had to get it for you. Cost, schmost, I just want you to be happy!"
- "Open it, I love it when you manage to get your face to move with joy."
- "Hey, that's what friends are for. Wheel up here and give me a hug!"
- "No restaurant! Everyone to my house; I've been cooking Grandma's cat recipe all day for you guys."
- "Of course you can bring the kids. Who doesn't like children for dessert?"

Here are holiday phrases you *do* hear at my house:

- To my assistant: "Stop staring at me, asshole. Grab a needle and start picking out that monogram. Regifting starts now."
- To my maid: "For the last time, dunce-face, put the iron on medium; otherwise you can't get the creases out and I can't reuse

wrapping paper or it will look like your thighs."

- "Don't open the door, Cooper! Just tell the doorman to leave it in the lobby, otherwise I'll have to give him a big Christmas tip and pretend to care that he's working while his children, Juan, Juanette, Juanacita and Juanita, are sitting around their plastic manger, missing Papa."
- "Here comes the Christmas special Meals on Wheels truck again. Get in bed quick, Melissa; they're starting to get suspicious."

DECEMBER 6

Dear Diary:

I'm sitting on a plane to Houston, traveling to do yet another benefit for Rodeo Clowns Without Partners, and I just had a brilliant idea for holiday shopping: *SkyMall*, the catalog that comes in the back of the airplane seats. They have *great* stuff, something for everyone, from hammocks to Crock-Pots to stereos to dildos. I'll bet I could even find something for Sienna Miller—which isn't easy; what do you buy for the woman who's had everyone?

DECEMBER 7

Dear Diary:

> December 7, 1941—a date which will live in infamy.
>
> —FRANKLIN DELANO ROOSEVELT

I've never been sure if FDR said that because that morning the Japanese attacked Pearl Harbor or because that afternoon he walked in on Eleanor up to her elbows in her cleaning lady. I'd prefer to think he was referring to Pearl Harbor. It's a less upsetting visual.

Going to D.C. tonight for some fancy-schmancy political dinner at the Four Seasons. I have always loved politics and have always been very active, going back to the Boston Tea Party. When all the Bostonians threw tea into the harbor, guess who brought the sugar?

DECEMBER 8

Dear Diary:

The dinner party in D.C. was fine and I think I looked great. I wanted to look like a woman familiar with politics and the politicians, so I dressed like a Beltway hooker. I was seated between two senators, and God were they stupid! I asked one how he thought we could get out of Iraq. He said, "Do what I do. Just leave some money on the bureau and sneak out while they're sleeping." I realized then and there that intelligence to a senator is like heterosexuality to RuPaul: impossible.

DECEMBER 9

Dear Diary:

I'm back in L.A. for a meeting with the Muppet people. I'm doing a QVC promo with Miss Piggy. I love Miss Piggy; she's worth a billion dollars! Pretty good deal for a fake pig with a hand up her ass.

DECEMBER 10

Dear Diary:

I went holiday shopping on Rodeo Drive today and thought I'd stop in at the Olive Garden for a quick bite. There was a big fat guy on line with his equally porcine wife right in front of me. I walked up to the hostess to ask her how long the wait would be. Suddenly, he yelled, "Hey, we're all waiting here, sister. Don't use that celebrity thing to cut the line." I was shocked. I *never ever ever* use the "celebrity thing" unless it's an absolute emergency such as being late for a mani-pedi. I tried to explain to him that I was simply asking the hostess a question, but he turned away, so I said to her, loud enough for Colossus to hear, "Is there any chance I could be seated right now? I'm a celebrity and if I have to wait for my table until after Tubby McShit is seated and has ordered, I'm afraid your Bottomless Pasta Bowl will have to change its name." She said, "Of course, Miss Rivers, right this way." As I was walking past Mr. Oink, I said, "Don't worry, Pork Rib, there will be plenty left for you; I won't be ordering the slop."

DECEMBER 11

Dear Diary:

I'm exhausted. It's the holiday season and I'm totally into the spirit. I spent the entire morning working with Melissa on a charity drive in Beverly Hills. And I am so proud to say Melissa and I alone collected over a thousand pounds of caviar for the needy in Palm Beach. And although some people say that our fund-raising was a bit hypocritical, we also threw a terrific cocktail party to raise funds for the Betty Ford Center. Below is a list of little-known charities that deserve national recognition:

- Charity for terminally ill gay children: the Make-A-Swish Foundation.
- Charity for children with chronic diarrhea: Toys for Trots (which is an offshoot of the charity for underprivileged Hindu children, Toys for Dots, and the one for rich society brats, Toys for Snots).

I'm a giver.

DECEMBER 12

Dear Diary:

Rumor has it that Adele complained that I did a joke about her being heavy on *Fashion Police*, and her lawyer wants a written apology that will say, "Dear Adele, I am truly sorry if my words, spoken in jest, have in any way upset you, offended you or hurt your family. I think you're a wonderful singer and artist and have brought joy and happiness to millions of people around the world. And you are not in any way heavy; in fact, little lady, you're slim, lithe and winsome." I told the lawyer that unfortunately I've run out of stationery, but I'd be delighted to write this long apology and that she's not obese where there's plenty of room for it—on her big fat ass.

What's all the fuss about? If a celebrity is fat, chances are it's because they want to be fat—it's part of their "look" and they're using it to make a fortune. Melissa McCarthy is brilliant; Rebel Wilson is hilarious—and both of those plus-sized gals are using their heft to pull in hefty salaries. Even Kirstie Alley, the sensitive Scientologist who hates being made fun of, had no problem doing a series called *Fat Actress*, so long as her paycheck matched her calorie count.

DECEMBER 13

Dear Diary:

Just watched TMZ and the big story of the day? Charles Manson is engaged! As they say in the *New York Post*'s "Page Six," "Yes, THAT Charles Manson." Apparently Chuckie's met a woman and fallen in love. I am so jealous! Not that I'd ever even think of marrying him. I'm Jewish and he thinks he's Jesus. But still . . . we're about the same age, yet Charlie, who lives in an eight-by-ten cell and showers once a week—with other men—has found someone, and I, who lives in a large apartment and goes to the theater nightly, am all alone. I may not be gorgeous, but for God's sake, when I have my face carved up it's done by a doctor and the scars are behind my ears, not on my forehead. Life is just not fair. I don't know if I'll be invited to the wedding but I hear they're registered at Bed Bloodbath & Beyond.

P.S. The fiancée, a woman known as "Star," looks just like Susan Atkins, the late psycho who killed Sharon Tate. Star's twenty-five, has brown hair, brown eyes and an X carved into her head. It's nice to know Charlie has a "type."

DECEMBER 14

Dear Diary:

I'm going through that wonderful *SkyMall* catalog yet again, and I'm finding fabulous Christmas gifts. They have two whole pages dedicated to garden gnomes! How wonderful for my Mexican gardener, Jose. How many times can I give him a piñata filled with breath mints? Jose is Mexican, and might I remind you, the Mexicans are not a tall people. Now he won't feel lonely as he mows.

DECEMBER 15

Dear Diary:

As I'm totally still into the Christmas mood, I went shopping today at that famous toy store FAO Schwarz. I went with one of my gayest gay BFFs, Jason. We walked in and there was Santa, sitting on a huge chair with a hundred kids waiting on line to sit on his lap and tell him what they wanted for Christmas. Jason joined them and when it was his turn, he jumped onto Santa's lap just like the kids, happily bouncing up and down. When Santa said, "So, young man, what do you want for Christmas?" Jason said, "Don't worry about it, fat boy. I'm getting it."

DECEMBER 16

Dear Diary:

I did an LGBT (Lesbians, Gays, Bisexuals, Transgender) benefit tonight. Show went great but the after-party was really interesting. They all seem to hate each other.

The lesbians hate the gay men because the gay men are pretty and giggly and well dressed and fun. The gays hate the lesbians because they're not. They both hate the bisexuals because they think bisexuals are nothing more than homos who think that "bi" makes them sound European and taller. And they all hate the trannies because they muck up the LGB fund-raising pool. Wealthy donors don't donate if they can't figure out what the fuck their money is going to.

I also learned that trannies don't like to be called "trannies." They take themselves very seriously and prefer the medical term "gash jockey."*

DECEMBER 17

Dear Diary:

Too busy to write today—I have to go to City Hall where Pingpong is applying for U.S. citizenship. She needed somebody to show up *in person* to attest to her good character and steady employment in the United States. I told her that as long as she covered her wrists and arms so the handcuff scars and radiator burns didn't show, I'd be more than happy to be her witness. Being of service like this makes me proud to be an American.

DECEMBER 18

Dear Diary:

Went to a very formal dinner party, and of all things I was seated next to a doctor who does transsexual operations. I told him I had done the LGBT benefit and he said many of his patients were there. Turns out he was a Nobel Prize winner who was known for both his penis deletions and labia load-ins. Over the most delicious pheasant-under-glass and wonderful Chateau Marmont

* The British medical term is "cooz-dick."

’53, I asked him, “C’mon, Doc, tell me, does a new penis really look like a penis? Does it work? Or are these guys just happy to have something slapping against their thighs?” He moved to another table.

DECEMBER 19

Dear Diary:

I’m starting to get depressed but not because of the holidays. All of my friends are in really good spaces in their lives and it’s killing me. I don’t have one friend who’s suffering, in financial distress or sexually confused. When I get off the phone with someone I want to be able to say, “Well, at least *I* don’t have to sell my house and live in a box” or “Thank God *my* second husband didn’t leave me for a small Romanian houseboy named Chechy” or “*I’m* not the one with no health insurance and a boil on my lip the size of Cleveland.” These are the phone calls that make me feel good when I’m blue.

I’m thinking of taking one of my gay AA friends* out drinking and encouraging him to have unprotected sex with Haitian street hustlers. Then, when I get his teary call of regret in the morning, I won’t feel so bad about gaining two pounds.

---

* He was a really bad alcoholic. In his day, he saw more ice than Peggy Fleming.

DECEMBER 20

Dear Diary:

Getting ready to go back to Mexico for the holidays. I've got to get industrial bug spray, a magnum of Imodium and $50,000 in cash to pay the ransom when a drug cartel kidnaps me because I had the effrontery to step sixteen inches outside of our compound walls.

DECEMBER 21

Dear Diary:

I am so tired of the homeless. They are always asking for things like food and shelter. Food, okay—I've always got a couple of Doritos in my pockets. But shelter? What am I supposed to do? Bring Mr. Stinko into my guest room? What if Michelle Obama drops by and wants to use it as a love nest for a clandestine tryst with Bill O'Reilly? Yes, Michelle! Who knows what goes on behind closed White House doors? There is so much sex in Washington, the house whip is leather.

Anyhow, back to the homeless. I have several questions I ask myself about them. I am very aware of them, as I see them daily while I'm carried from my foyer to my limo.

QUESTION 1: Why are there no pretty homeless? God knows they have time to fix themselves up; they don't work. No roof should not mean no makeup. There is no direct correlation between physical beauty and housing. Halle Berry was on food stamps, while Eleanor Roosevelt lived in the White House. I rest my case.

QUESTION 2: Why do the homeless just lie there and beg? You want money? Make a fucking effort. I'll happily toss you a couple of shekels, but do a little trick for me—juggle, tell a joke, pretend you're in the talent competition in the Miss America Pageant and do a dramatic reading of *The Cat in the Hat*. There's one guy in my neighborhood who stands on the corner with a picture frame around his neck telling people, "I've been framed." I always give him money—clever idea and funnier than 37 percent of my act. There's another guy on the corner of Fifty-Eighth and Madison who's been singing "Ave Maria" for years. I always give him money. I'd give him more if he had a better arrangement.

QUESTION 3: What's with the shopping carts? Haven't you moved past that yet? Get a Valpak or a suitcase or buy online like everyone else. Shopping carts are so 1983. For God's sake, catch up!

LAST QUESTION: Why do charitable organizations always say "Feed the Homeless"? The homeless don't need food; the fatter they get, the more they'll have to cover in cold weather. As a matter of fact, they have plenty of food—there's a Dumpster on every corner. (Freddie once told me that if it weren't for Dumpster diving he never would've met Nick Nolte!)

DECEMBER 22

Dear Diary:

On the plane to Mexico where I'll meet Melissa, Cooper, my one friend, and hangers-on.

DECEMBER 23

Dear Diary:

I'm glad I'm in Mexico for the holidays. In New York, I get depressed because everyone's coupled up and I'm all alone. I've never appealed to men, not even my husband, Edgar. The only compliment he ever gave me was, "Joan, in bed you're like Marilyn Monroe. Dead." The only way I can get a man to touch me these days is if I walk through the casino where I'm performing and say, "Hey, high roller, wanna rub me for luck?" I hate to complain, but I have to face it, I have no sex appeal. I've yet to find a gynecologist who has the nerve to examine me twice.

DECEMBER 24

Dear Diary:

Got my first Christmas gift today from Melissa and Cooper: a beautiful diamond-studded sombrero. They hid it in a place I'd never look—the kitchen. Melissa and Cooper spent a lot of money and it's making me rethink my gift-spending policy. I always believed that I should give till it hurts, but I find that my pain threshold is about a buck fifty these days. Which reminds me, I haven't bought them anything and I better hurry. As Winona Ryder called to remind me: There's only one shoplifting day left until Christmas.

DECEMBER 25

Dear Diary:

Christmas in Mexico is terrific. The people are so inventive. They don't waste money on decorations. If they want something red and green in their living rooms, they just go out and steal a traffic light.

Yes, yes, I know we're Jewish, but I still think Christmas is the best holiday of all. I make my Nativity scene a Jewish-Christian event. For example, I have the three wise men bringing Jesus their gifts: gold, frankincense and Myrna, Beverly Hills' most famous hooker. Speaking of Jesus, I had him in a manger, but being Jewish I put an electric blanket in with him. And when it comes to Mary, I have a beautiful little figurine, but instead of that blue schmata she usually wears, I dressed her in a Chanel suit, Manolo Blahnik shoes and a Gucci bag. The way I feel is: You're the mother of God. Look it!

DECEMBER 26

Dear Diary:

Melissa got me a new diary for Christmas. What is she, crazy?? I hate it!!! I think I'm going to go knock on her door and really upset her. I'm going to strip naked and say, "Surprise! This is what you're going to look like in twenty years!"

DECEMBER 27

Dear Diary:

I have no idea where the staff has gone. I didn't want to insult them by giving them monetary gifts for Christmas, so instead I gave them big hugs and wished them all "Feliz Navidad." They, in turn, gave me the finger.

DECEMBER 28

Dear Diary:

Not a good day. I got the runs. I was on the toilet so long my ass took root.

DECEMBER 29

Dear Diary:

Still sick. I've thrown up so much I feel like I could audition for the lead in *The Nicole Richie Story*.

DECEMBER 30

Dear Diary:

Getting ready for New Year's Eve. A lot of people get nostalgic at the end of the year, and they like to reminisce about old times. Not me. As a matter of fact, I always refuse to join in the singing of "Auld Lang Syne." If I want to sing a classic old song, it won't be "Auld Lang Syne." I'll sing a classic old song that speaks to me, like "Money Makes the World Go Round" or "Push, Push in the Bush."

DECEMBER 31

Dear Diary:

It's New Year's Eve and the five of us left here in Mexico who haven't died from dysentery are making our New Year's resolutions. I make the same three resolutions every single year:

1. Only make faces at blind people.
2. Tell crying orphans to suck it up. Nobody wants to hear them whine. Nobody wants them, period; that's why they're orphans.

3. Lose weight. I love to eat. I bought a picture of the Last Supper just to look at the food.

Anyway, it's almost midnight in New York and we're all heading to the living room to watch the ball drop and watch Anderson Cooper and Kathy Griffin ring in 2014. It's one of the best moments of the year. But I'm always hoping that a huge gust of wind (from Dr. Phil's ass) will come along at 11:59 and blow Kathy and Anderson off the roof and into the Hudson River. So, at this time next year, Melissa and I could be on top of that building dropping the ball and counting down to 2015! Wow!

Happy New Year!!!!

Just got a call from my publisher, Zelda Gonifsky—she said she's not happy with the book. Zelda said, "Girlchick, I need something more scandalous. I had no idea you led such a boring life." This killed me as Zellie herself was calling me from a ChristianMingle bingo parlor during Jell-O break.

Zelda continued, "Joan! For the paperback I need more bang for my buck!"

I said, "Z! You want more bang for your buck? Great. How about I come out in favor of school shootings? Is that a big enough bang for you?"

She said, "Is that true?"

I said, "I'm just kidding. What's wrong with you? Do you work for TMZ?"

She said, "Joanie, I finally read the fucker and there were a couple of days when you didn't make *any* diary entries. I don't know why—maybe you were busy with your scheme of breeding pit bulls with cocker spaniels so after they've killed somebody you'll forgive them because of their big eyes, or maybe you were trying to rescue some attractive trapped miners, whatever . . . But if anything juicy happened on those days I think it would really help paperback sales." Then she yelled, "For God's sake, I just want the truth!"

I yelled back, "You can't handle the truth!"

Then she said the five words that make the world go round: Not "I believe in one God"; they were, "There will be no check."

I started to write.

THE TRUTH

FEBRUARY 28

Dear Diary:

I woke up this morning, naked and bruised in the back of Brad Pitt's Maserati. He, George Clooney and Bradley Cooper apparently slipped a roofie into my applesauce while I was visiting orphans rejected by the Smile Foundation and then rented my comatose body out to prisoners on death row. I remember very little although the last words I heard were: "Wow! Not one of those guys—even though they were going to die tomorrow—had their way with Granny. As a matter of fact, three of them who were up for appeal took one look at her and dropped it."

MARCH 14

Dear Diary:

I hate the term "trending." It's nothing more than a synonym for "what's hot" or a word that noncreative television executives use instead of "what kind of cheap garbage can we sell to a fourteen-year-old today?"

In 1937, anti-Semitism was "trending." In 1944, polio was "trending" (FDR was just ahead of the curve). In 2009, making sex tapes with black men was "trending."

You know what's "trending" now? Publishers who

want to bleed another chapter out of their authors, most of who moved on to other projects six months ago.

MARCH 15

Dear Diary:

Guess what else is trending. Cocktail parties where A-list celebrities who are now D-list celebrities wait on you for (tax-free) tips. I went to one of those parties last night at Leo DiCaprio's house and left early because it was very upsetting. (Not as upsetting as when I found out that Susan Boyle and I have the same plastic surgeon, but upsetting nonetheless.) I know *Mamma Mia!* didn't do the numbers the studio thought it would but it really broke my heart to have Meryl Streep offer me a napkin, and murmur, "Excuse me, ma'am—would you like to try the mini quiche? The cook says the chutney is invigorating!" I said, "No thanks." Five minutes later a dark-haired waitress with a Polish accent, a major mole and a limp offered me the same thing. When I took it she pulled off her wig and screamed, "Fooled you! It's me, Meryl! See! I've still got it! Please, tell some producer."

I thought I'd be fine at Leo's party, but I was wrong—and not just because Michael Bolton scratched my car while he was parking it, but because no one was interested in what I was saying. And why? It was the same old Hollywood story.

All the successful men, instead of talking with me, were vying to talk to a bunch of gorgeous supermodels who were hanging out near the ladies' room waiting for their turn to purge. All of the girls' names ended in *ie* with little hearts over the *i*'s. There was Bambie, Tiffanie, Maryie, Susie, Cathie, Kathie and Shaniquie. I listened in so I could find out what these girls were saying that had the mogul men's rapt attention:

"Hello. Did you know there are two *l*'s in 'hello'?"
"I gained a quarter of a pound last year. Wanna touch where?"
"I didn't know Stevie Wonder was blind. I thought he just liked Ray-Bans."
"I consider my dog my child but, of course, I didn't give birth to him."
"Barack Obama . . . sounds familiar. Is he in a band?"

I finally walked away when I got a text from Bill Gates. I thought, "Well, at least one man appreciates a woman for her mind and her accomplishments." Bill texted:

This is Bill Gates. We met in the kitchen about an hour ago. You're the smartest woman at the party. I had to meet you. I figured you would know Bambie's phone number.

APRIL 4

Dear Diary:

My gift to Amy Winehouse was just returned. What a selfish bitch. It was such a thoughtful present—Pingpong put in a lot of time and energy researching and shopping (online). I got Amy a lifetime subscription to the Israeli *Playboy*—it's called: *If You Fix Your Nose You'll Be Gorgeous.*

APRIL 9

Dear Diary:

Had lunch with my lawyer Murray "the Gonif" Madoff. In the middle of pushing my food around my plate so the other bulimics in the restaurant would think I was eating, the Gonif blurted out, "Joan, what's the one thing you want to do after you retire?"

I said, "Why should I retire?"

He said, "Lately you're urinating onstage and it's becoming very distracting for the first six rows."

I said, "Point well taken. How about I cut back on the cranberry juice?"

"Fine," he said, "but until the plan kicks in, stop eating asparagus."

But Murray's question did get me thinking about the one thing *other* celebrities should do when they retire . . .

- Gwyneth Paltrow should travel the world and have nobody recognize her. (Oh wait, that's happening now.)

- Diana Ross should learn to be sorta nice to people and no longer slap the disabled.
- Anderson Cooper should teach his boyfriend to be gentle. "It's a penis, Jose, not a handle."
- Sharon Stone should only wear crotchless Spanx so she can flash the old men in her nursing home. "C'mon, Grandpas! Time for *Leave It to Beaver*!"

MAY 18

Dear Diary:

I always get patriotic around certain big holidays—the Fourth of July, Labor Day, Veterans Day, Oprah's birthday . . .

Last night I was watching a documentary about our Founding Fathers and I decided that there are two things I hate about the Declaration of Independence.

I hate the stationery it's written on. Parchment was only trending for a few months and then was never used again except for the menus at Caesars Palace in Las Vegas. And two: I hate that I can't read a lot of it as the handwriting is lousy. I realize that quills are a tad unwieldy but still, the doctors who created my chin shouldn't have better penmanship than the men who created our democracy.

I also hate both the Constitution and the Bill of Rights. They're so wishy-washy. The preamble to the Constitution starts out with "We the people . . ." What people? Who? I want names! My aunt Lea? It takes her an hour to pick a ripe cantaloupe; I'm going to trust her with foreign policy?

And what they grant us is so wrong. Take, for example, that Freedom of Speech stuff. I think Freedom of Speech should be limited as far as all female comedians go, except for me. (I don't care what Sarah Silverman says; she must be silenced once and for all. The bitch already took three club dates from me this month alone.)

Someone needs to tell Michelle Obama and all of CNN's newscasters: It's the Right to Bear Arms, not "bare" arms. Wear sleeves, girls. Enough is enough. This goes double for women over fifty-five who are members of Hadassah.

The Freedom of Religion bit is fine, but only in certain parts of the country. I don't like to walk into a room and see one man kneeling before another man unless it's in West Hollywood.

As for the Bill of Rights, I'd like to create my Bill of Rights for *today*, not some stupid bill that allows me to carry a musket if I see redcoats coming. (If I ever end up seeing redcoats coming, it will be at Fashion Week, and I won't be carrying a musket. I'll be carrying a ticket to Valentino's private after-party.)

The numero uno right in my new bill would be a Right to Hire Illegals. I truly believe that if you make more than $100,000 a year and pay over 20 percent in taxes you should be able to hire as many illegals who are sturdy enough to tunnel in as you want. They make excellent staff members and, on occasion, elegant side tables. Tawny-colored skin takes a Pledge shine beautifully.

I would insist on a right for the nonhandicapped to be allowed to park in handicapped spots and not have to pretend to walk funny because somebody's watching them. This ruined two gorgeous pairs of Manolos for me last week alone.

I would modify the Right to Assembly so that it excludes any Justin Bieber concert. I'd love to see that runty little midget come out and sing "Baby, Baby, Baby" into a dead mic. And I'd amend the Right to Search and Seizure to include a "before the third date" clause. Let's get back to American values. This would enable slightly homely women to get a couple of free dinners before they had to put out.

We should have the Right to Mock the Mildly Autistic without having to listen to their parents tell us how talented they are in strange ways: "Little Jimmy can play the 'Minute Waltz' in fourteen seconds" or "Bonnie can retouch the Masters perfectly with crayons and modeling clay" or "My Amy made *The Guinness Book of World Records* for hopping indoors in place. We had to move, but we're so proud."

I would be more specific as to what is cruel and unusual punishment. I'm the first to agree that waterboarding is bad to a point, but not cruel and unusual punishment. Making some jihad terrorist-bomb-strapper-on-er watch a Jennifer Aniston movie every time they come up for air? *That's* cruel and unusual punishment.

I'd get rid of the crap about a "trial by a jury of peers." There's no such thing as a "jury of peers." Why do you think the O. J. verdict went south? It was impossible for that dumb, chinless Marcia Clark to find twelve black Heisman Trophy winners who'd slaughtered their wives while wearing expensive gloves and size-ten Bruno Magli loafers. I'd get rid of "trial by jury," period. I'd replace it with "trial by Judge Judy." Not only will she come to the right decision *every* time, but she'll apply the death penalty if you cross your arms and chew gum.

Which leads me to a big one: the Right to Vote. What moron decided everyone should be allowed to vote? People should only do what they're good at doing. You don't ask the Elephant Man for beauty tips. You don't ask Mrs. Duggar, "What's your favorite condom?" If you can't read the ballot without moving your lips you shouldn't be allowed to vote. Following is a list of people who should not be allowed to vote:

- People who have children under four who weigh more than a hundred pounds.
- People who have houses with wheels.
- People who mispronounce "ask" as "ax" when they're not discussing Lizzie Borden.
- People who carry guns that don't light cigarettes or blow bubbles.
- People who write the words "Your Name" on applications where it says, "Your name here."
- People whose IQ is lower than their neck measurement.

- People who would pay full price to see Jay Leno, the Osmonds or televangelists wearing jewelry worth more than your house.

MAY 26

Dear Diary:

Went to a cookout for veterans. I love veterans—we have so much in common: They have Purple Hearts, I have purple veins. They fought the Nazis at Omaha Beach in World War II; I bitch-slapped Heidi Klum when she spit out my kugel at Mel Gibson's Save the Non-Jewish Children Bake Sale.

My cousin Seymour "Three Fingers" Lefkowitz claims he's a veteran and loves to talk about how he was injured during the "Big One."* Not only is Seymour chatty about his inability to buy gloves off the rack, he's the polar opposite of most of the disfigured, who have the decency and grace to hide their focus-pulling stumps so the rest of us may finish our dinners without incident (and without fear of staring or vomiting). But Cousin Seymour can't show off his mangled paw often enough. In fact, he uses his three-finger infirmity to great advantage: Not only is he able to win bowling tournaments, but he's also able to score with the homely-but-still-better-looking-

* World War II is always referred to as the "Big One." I did some research and found out that World War I is known as the "Biggish One," Vietnam is known as the "Longer Than It Is Big One" and Iraq is known as the "What the Fuck Are We Doing Here? One."

than-he-is women at synagogues and nonrestricted country clubs all over the tristate area. Seymour, who is a bit confused by actual dates, tells everyone that he lost his fingers in a battle in Germany, in the Ardennes, pulling a grenade out of the vagina of a pretty, young Princess Diana who had fallen down in a minefield trying to outrun a panzer division. The truth of the matter is that the closest Seymour has ever gotten to war was spending the entire Korean conflict* "stationed" in an Army accounting office in Weehawken, New Jersey, where he lost his pinkie and pointer in a freak calculator mishap. Even though Seymour is a liar he's no dummy; women love heroes. Nobody wants to fuck an actuary.

• • •

Note:

Not happily (as there will be no added compensation) I am adding this entry to the paperback version of the book at the "request" of my elevator man Ray, who is highly offended that I have neglected/forgotten/didn't give a shit about/or even worse purposely left town on his birthday, August 3, and therefore didn't make an entry. So, in order to hear the elevator stop once again at my floor when I ring the bell, here goes:

---

* Remember that one? My Korean nail girl, Maly, certainly does. I think she purposely cuts my cuticles too short every time I go in for the $7.99 special, saying, "Vely solly, ugry white rady. I still got shakes from when Amelican bomb hit my virrage." I say nothing but my displeasure is reflected in the tip.

AUGUST 3

Dear Diary:

It's my favorite elevator man Ray's birthday. He is always so cheerful with his "Good morning" as I step into the elevator, even though he works the afternoon shift. But frankly, I am so happy to be out of town on his special day as it would mean a bigger tip.

Cooper and I just landed in some small airport in the middle of nowhere—this place is emptier than the theater at a Pat Boone concert. The minute I got off the plane there was an e-mail from Ray, a tad upset that I didn't leave him a present. Ray, I e-mailed back. Don't worry. The incontinent lady in 4C will be leaving you a present in a few minutes.

Actually, Ray was more than a "tad" upset. Here was his reply:

> Yo, Jew bitch. Today is my birfday and you done forget it and took that boy wit you to see da' heartland. Funny, cuz' you ain't got no heart. I hope when you gets back you remember I be da' one who help you with packages and groceries and shit, not 2 mention the death threats, stink bombs and ticking boxes that come 4 you evry friggin' day.

This e-mail amazed me as (1) Ray is a Long Island (*pronounced Lawng Oy-lend*)–born Ph.D. from the University of Oslo, and (2) this is why I really should *only* hire illegals.

I have no leverage with Ray. What am I going to do, threaten to deport him back to Roslyn Heights?

Anyway, why fight? Here is my special birthday message to Ray: *Happy Birthday, Ray! I hope this diary entry will, in some small way, make up for the severe emotional trauma I have caused you by having the effrontery to take my sallow, slightly malnourished grandson on a vacation before I die from decrepitude and old age on your special day. I don't know what I was thinking. I shall make it up to you at Christmas when I will fill your stocking with much much more than my usual $3 holiday tip. I hope you got all you deserved on your special day; and I'm sure the testicular itching will clear up soon.*

AUGUST 25

Later that day . . .

Dear Diary:

Just heard from my agent Steve Levine's lawyer. He wants an apology. Seriously?

Okay, Steve, gloves off!

Let's talk (1) about that "green date" you got me in Indianapolis where we split the cash fee fifty-fifty, under the table. Have you told the IRS? Because I plan to.

Let's talk (2) about that great imitation you do of your top client, Uma Thurman, when she's not in the room. I think she'd be fascinated to see the wig, boots, lashes and flat putty nose you don whenever you do her famous "I think I've got a yeast infection" bit. Should I call Tarantino and give him a heads-up?

And (3) how about your Mafia connection? Vinnie "the Chin" Gigante may be gone, but everyone knows—or will know—that Milton "Kiss My Prostate" Lubetkin is your personal bagman.

So you'd better rethink that lawsuit, Stevie boy; this canary's got big, Botoxed lips.

SEPTEMBER 24

Dear Diary:

Just got another letter from someone who wants to sue me. This time it's from George Michael and it was on very stained paper. George took umbrage at my September 8 entry. He wants an apology. He says what I wrote is absolutely not true (see page 191). He says due to age, arthritis and general wear and tear from years of trying to sneak under stalls in public men's rooms he can no longer bend, let alone get on his knees. He even enclosed a doctor's note—also on very stained paper. Okay, fine, I apologize, George. George is a wonderful man, a great entertainer and I hope that things go well so that George can have a little naked fun without having to strain his lower torso. Georgie is, as they say in Scotland, a wee laddie so I pray that one day he and Shaquille O'Neal will have a face-to-crotch meeting.

• • •

I am *very* upset. Again. Just heard from my publisher, Zelda, with the final financial tally on my last book, *I Hate Everyone . . . Starting with Me.* Even though it was on the *New York Times* bestsellers list for weeks and weeks, was translated into twenty-seven languages (including Farsi, Arabic and Esperanto)—the paperback and eBook sales went through the roof—not only were all the profits eaten up but apparently I owe Penguin $276.43. Something about legal fees. As I walked out of Zelda's office I overheard her severely hearing-impaired intern whisper, "POOR BITCH MADE NO MONEY ON HER BOOK. ALL WENT TO LAWYERS."

Fuck her, too.

Please send all hate mail to my editor, Hermione Schwartz, at the Berkley Publishing Group. You can look up the fucking address yourself. If you have the time to write a stupid letter, you have the time to go through a phone book.

THE *NEW YORK TIMES* BESTSELLER

Joan Rivers, comedienne, actress, jewelry monger, and an award-winning international star lived by the golden rule: Do unto others before they do unto you—and for God's sakes, do it funny!

Here—uncensored and uninhibited—Joan says exactly what's on her mind. She lets everyone, including herself, have it in this one hundred percent honest and unabashedly hilarious love letter to the hater in all of us.

"More punch lines per paragraph than any book I've read in years."
—*The New York Times*

"She holds nothing back." —*The Washington Post*

"Often hilarious, often shocking, totally politically incorrect." —Liz Smith

joan.co
penguin.com

BERKLEY | Penguin Random House

T470-0215